ACKEST NIGHT

GEOFF JOHNS
WRITER

IVAN REIS
PENCILLER

OCLAIR ALBERT
INKER

ROB HUNTER	PROLOGUE
JULIO FERREIRA	PART TWO
JOE PRADO	PARTS THREE—EIGHT
ADDITIONAL INKS	

ALEX SINCLAIR
COLORIST

NICK J. NAPOLITANO
LETTERER

IVAN REIS & OCLAIR ALBERT
with **ALEX SINCLAIR**
COVERS

Eddie Berganza Editor-original series / Adam Schlagman Associate Editor-original series
Robbin Brosterman Design Director – Books

Bob Harras Senior VP – Editor-in-Chief, DC Comics

Diane Nelson President / Dan DiDio and Jim Lee Co-Publishers / Geoff Johns Chief Creative Officer
John Rood Executive VP – Sales, Marketing and Business Development / Amy Genkins Senior VP – Business and
Legal Affairs / Nairi Gardiner Senior VP – Finance / Jeff Boison VP – Publishing Planning / Mark Chiarello VP – Art
Direction and Design / John Cunningham VP – Marketing / Terri Cunningham VP – Editorial Administration
Alison Gill Senior VP – Manufacturing and Operations / Hank Kanalz Senior VP – Vertigo and Integrated Publishing
Jay Kogan VP – Business and Legal Affairs, Publishing / Jack Mahan VP – Business Affairs, Talent / Nick Napolitano
VP – Manufacturing Administration / Sue Pohja VP – Book Sales / Courtney Simmons Senior VP – Publicity
Bob Wayne Senior VP – Sales

Cover by Ivan Reis with Rodolfo Migliari

DC COMICS 1700 Broadway, New York, NY 10019 A Warner Bros. Entertainment Company

Printed by Transcontinental Interglobe, Beauceville, QC, Canada. 10/11/13. Fourth Printing. ISBN: 978-1-4012-2953-5

Library of Congress Cataloging-in-Publication Data

Johns, Geoff, 1973- author.

Blackest Night / Geoff Johns, Ivan Reis, Oclair Albert, Joe Prado.

pages cm

"Originally published in single magazine form in Blackest Night 0-8."

ISBN 978-1-4012-2953-5

1. Graphic novels. I. Reis, Ivan, illustrator. II. Albert, Oclair, illustrator. III. Prado, Joe, illustrator. IV. Title.

PN6728.G742J64 2013

741.5'973–dc23

2012045995

INTRODUCTION

by Donald De Line

It's 2 am, and I'm standing in a deserted alleyway in New Orleans. Ominous shadows fall across the brick buildings—not the kind of neighborhood where you want to find yourself alone at night. But thankfully, I'm not. Cast and crew buzz about, preparing for the shot, making final adjustments, getting everything just right. With lights rigged, cameras set and actors positioned, our director Martin Campbell shouts *action*. For the first time we see Ryan Reynolds as Hal Jordan embrace his destiny. Wielding the iconic ring, he wreaks havoc against a dark force. I think to myself: "Geoff is really going to love this!"

To give a little context, we are on day two of shooting the motion picture *Green Lantern*. It took a lot of hard work to arrive at this moment, and I must say it feels great to see the cameras rolling. It is a complex and difficult endeavor bringing a story of this scope to life, and we would never be here if not for our creative partner and comic book godfather, Geoff Johns, whose GREEN LANTERN: SECRET ORIGIN is the touchstone for our film. Along with SECRET ORIGIN, Geoff's vision for Green Lantern gave us REBIRTH and then SINESTRO CORPS WAR, but these two series were merely setting the stage for this seminal work: BLACKEST NIGHT.

During my career in film, I've seen how difficult it can be to bring a fresh interpretation to an intellectual property rich in history and tradition. In the case of Green Lantern, we are talking about a character that has been in existence for some 70 years. Yet Geoff has pulled off this feat with aplomb. BLACKEST NIGHT is a groundbreaking culmination of his efforts with artist Ivan Reis. The eight-issue series has taken Green Lantern to unprecedented places, breathing new life and energy into the storied mythology. The result of Geoff and Ivan's vision is something special that the devoted Green Lantern fan base—as well as future generations of Green Lantern fans—can embrace.

In BLACKEST NIGHT, Geoff and Ivan have preserved the signature qualities that made us fall in love with Green Lantern in the first place. At the same time, the series weaves a complete narrative that repositions Green Lantern at the forefront of the DC Universe. Not content with rejuvenating merely the Green Lantern Corps, Geoff creates a story that brings all of the DC characters together, illustrating their greatest powers and weaknesses to save the universe from destruction. In doing so, BLACKEST NIGHT embraces certain lesser-known characters, giving them exciting new identities. By bestowing rings on these characters, for both good and evil, Geoff has brought the Green Lantern universe into uncharted territory.

From an artistic standpoint, BLACKEST NIGHT features the brilliant work of Ivan Reis, whose visceral illustrations imbue the world with a newfound gravitas. Ivan's detailed artwork is terrifyingly lifelike, and is masterfully applied in introducing the black rings and raising the Black Lanterns. Beyond that, BLACKEST NIGHT is striking for the manner in which it grounds the characters with an emotional veracity upon seeing their loved ones and enemies raised from the dead. Heavy stuff, indeed, but the best work challenges you to ask difficult questions, while at the same time it thoroughly entertains. Geoff and Ivan have taken the vast Green Lantern mythos and given it their own spin, creating a series that is well deserving of the Eisner Award nomination.

When you consider Geoff and Ivan's careers on the whole, it is hard not to be impressed, and yet there's no reason to think their work won't continue to reach new heights moving forward. From a narrative standpoint, Geoff has taken this high-concept, cosmic idea and with the characters that we know and love, grounded it in reality. Making these extraordinary personalities relatable is the hallmark of great superhero writing. Above all, Geoff has earned our trust as an authority on all things Green Lantern.

Back on set, we are now three weeks into production. As we finish up Abin Sur's fateful crash scene, I get a buzz on my BlackBerry. It's Geoff, and he's just seen some early footage:

"Really, just blown away by it all."

The feeling's mutual, Geoff.

Donald De Line is a producer on the *Green Lantern* motion picture. He has also produced the films *The Italian Job*, *Body of Lies*, *Observe and Report* and *I Love You, Man*.

THE STORY SO FAR...

Billions of years ago, the self-appointed Guardians of the Universe recruited thousands of sentient beings from across the cosmos to join their intergalactic police force: the Green Lantern Corps.

Chosen because they are able to overcome great fear, the Green Lanterns patrol their respective space sectors armed with power rings capable of wielding the emerald energy of willpower into whatever constructs they can imagine.

Hal Jordan is the greatest of them all.

When the dying Green Lantern Abin Sur crashed on Earth, he chose Hal Jordan to be his successor, for his indomitable will and fearlessness. As the protector of Sector 2814, Hal has saved Earth from destruction, even died in its service and been reborn.

Thaal Sinestro of Korugar was once considered the greatest Green Lantern of them all.

As Abin Sur's friend, Sinestro became Jordan's mentor in the Corps. But after being sentenced to the Anti-Matter Universe for abusing his power, Sinestro learned of the yellow light of fear being mined on Qward. Wielding a new golden power ring fueled by terror, Sinestro drafted thousands of the most horrific, psychotic and sadistic beings in the universe, and with their doctrine of fear, burned all who opposed them.

When the Green Lantern Corps battled their former ally during the Sinestro Corps War, the skies burned with green and gold as Earth erupted into an epic battle between good and evil. Though the Green Lanterns won, their brotherhood was broken and the peace they achieved was short-lived. In its aftermath, the Guardians rewrote the Book of Oa, the very laws by which their corps abides, and dissent grew within their members.

Now Hal Jordan will face his greatest challenge yet, as the prophecy foretold by Abin Sur in his dying moments finally comes to pass...

The emotional spectrum has splintered into seven factions. Seven corps were born.

The Green Lanterns. The Sinestro Corps. Atrocitus and the enraged Red Lanterns. Larfleeze, the avaricious keeper of the Orange Light. Former Guardians Ganthet and Sayd's small but hopeful Blue Lantern Corps. The Zamarons and their army of fierce and loving Star Sapphires. And the mysterious Indigo Tribe.

As the War of Light ignited between these Lantern bearers, the skies on every world darkened. In Sector 666, on the planet Ryut, a black lantern grew around the Anti-Monitor's corpse, using his vast energies to empower it.

The first of the Black Lanterns, the Black Hand, has risen from the dead, heralding a greater power that will extinguish all of the light—and life—in the universe.

Now across thousands of worlds, the dead have risen, and Hal Jordan and all of Earth's greatest heroes must bear witness to Blackest Night, which will descend upon them all, without prejudice, mercy or reason.

THERE WAS *DARKNESS*.

THEN THERE WAS *LIGHT*.

AND THE *WAR* BETWEEN THEM BEGAN.

WHEN A DYING ALIEN GAVE ME A *RING* OF GREEN *WILL POWER*, IT BECAME *MY* JOB TO *BRIGHTEN* THE *BLACKEST* CORNERS OF SPACE.

RECENTLY, THAT'S GOTTEN A LITTLE MORE *COMPLICATED*.

I WAS A KID WHEN I LEARNED ABOUT THE *SPECTRUM* OF *COLORS*.

ANYONE OVER THE AGE OF *THREE* KNOWS IT.

R.O.Y.G.B.I.V.

I DIDN'T PAY ATTENTION TO IT. I WAS *NEVER* AN ARTIST.

I WAS JUST A GUY TRYING TO PROVE HE WASN'T *AFRAID*.

OF *ANYTHING*.

OR *ANYONE*.

THOMAS AND MARTHA WAYNE

MY NAME IS
HAL JORDAN.

I'M AN OFFICER OF
THE *GREEN LANTERN*
CORPS. SPACE
SECTOR 2814.

NO MATTER HOW
BRIGHTLY I SHINE MY
LIGHT TODAY, THE
SHADOWS WON'T
BE *LIFTED.*

BRUCE WAYNE...

...BATMAN...

I'M NOT *THREATENING* YOU, JORDAN, I'M *TELLING* YOU--

-- THE NEXT TIME YOU GIVE AWAY MY POSITION, *GLOWING* LIKE A DAMN *LIGHTNING BUG*--

--I'M GOING TO PUT THAT *RING* WHERE IT WON'T *SHINE.*

IT'S NOT *MY* FAULT *HIDING* IN THE SHADOWS IS YOUR ONLY "*SUPER-POWER.*"

ANOTHER REASON I *PREFER* BEING *UNDER-WATER.*

LESS *SHOUTING.*

...BATMAN IS DEAD.

FZZSH

HAL.

HAS ANYONE TOLD YOU WHAT KIND OF SERVICE *YOU* HAD WHEN YOU WERE *LOST* TO THE *SPEED FORCE?*

I HAVEN'T HAD TIME TO ASK.

YOU PACKED THE HOUSE, BARRY. PEOPLE CAME FROM EVERYWHERE. AND I DO MEAN *EVERYWHERE.*

THE FAR *FUTURE,* PARALLEL *WORLDS,* SUPER-INTELLIGENT *GORILLA* CITIES.

IT WAS THE EXACT *OPPOSITE* OF *MINE.*

WHEN I WAS INFECTED BY *PARALLAX,* DRIVEN *MAD* WITH *FEAR,* AND THEY THOUGHT *I* WAS *DEAD?*

MY TOMBSTONE WAS *DESECRATED.* NOT BY MY ENEMIES. BY OLD ALLIES.

I DIED A *SINNER.*

YOU DIED A *SAINT.*

THAT'S MY *POINT.* DEATH ISN'T NECESSARILY THE *END.* NOT IN *THIS* LINE OF WORK. YOU. ME. CLARK. OLLIE.

MY FATHER. YOUR MOTHER. THEY NEVER CAME BACK. NO MATTER HOW *HARD* WE WANTED THEM TO.

BUT SOMETHING'S *PRIED* THE DOOR *OPEN.* THERE'S A *BIGGER FORCE* AT WORK, THAT MUCH I BELIEVE.

AND IF THERE'S AN *ESCAPE,* YOU CAN BET *BATMAN'S* ALREADY *PLANNING* IT.

"BATMAN *ALWAYS* HAD A PLAN."

"WE'LL FIGURE IT OUT WHEN WE *GET* THERE"?

BE AN *OPTIMIST* FOR ONCE, BATMAN. WE'RE THE *JUSTICE LEAGUE--*

"-- WE'RE UNTOUCHABLE."

BATMAN WAS HIT BY DARKSEID'S *OMEGA BEAMS.*

SUPERMAN HELD HIS *SKELETON* IN HIS ARMS.

AND THEY *BURIED* HIM RIGHT HERE.

EVERYTHING *CHANGED* WHEN YOU *DISAPPEARED,* BARRY.

THE WORLD GOT MORE *DANGEROUS.*

OUR JOBS MORE *DEADLY.*

THE JUSTICE LEAGUE WASN'T *UNTOUCHABLE* ANYMORE.

"ARTHUR CURRY...

"...AQUAMAN...

"...HE WAS *KILLED* AFTER SPENDING *MONTHS* TRAPPED IN SOME KIND OF MUTATED STATE.

"THERE WERE RUMORS OF HIS RESURFACING DURING DARKSEID'S ATTACK--

"--BUT THEY WERE JUST THAT...

ARTHUR CURRY SON, HUSBAND and FATHER

"...RUMORS."

"J'ONN J'ONZZ...

"...MARTIAN MANHUNTER...

"...HE WAS *MURDERED* BY DARKSEID'S FOLLOWERS.

"HE'S BURIED ON MARS--

"--THE HEART AND SOUL OF THE JUSTICE LEAGUE IS GONE."

AND NOW SO IS *BRUCE.*

I MAY NOT HAVE TALKED WITH HIM *LATE* INTO THE NIGHT ABOUT *FORENSICS* AND *CRIMINAL PSYCHOLOGY* LIKE YOU...WE HAD OUR *DIFFERENCES,* PLENTY OF THEM...

"...BUT AFTER ALL WAS SAID AND DONE..."

YOU SAW THEM *DIE* IN FRONT OF YOU?

YES.

I DIDN'T KNOW. WHEN *I* WAS A KID--

YOU WATCHED A PLANE CRASH TAKE YOUR FATHER'S LIFE.

NO WONDER WE'RE BOTH SCREWED UP.

SPEAK FOR YOURSELF.

BRUCE WAS MY *FRIEND.*

THEY WERE *MY* FRIENDS *TOO,* HAL.

AND I WON'T STOP *HOPING* THAT THEY'LL FIND THEIR WAY BACK.

YES. *THIS* ONE.

"LIKE *YOU* AND I DID."

PART ONE

SOME THINGS ARE *WORSE* THAN *DEATH*...

...SOME THINGS...

...LIKE *ME.*

SPACE SECTOR 2814. GOTHAM CITY.

THE GRAVES OF THOMAS AND MARTHA WAYNE--

-- AND THE UNMARKED GRAVE OF THEIR SON, BRUCE.

KKK. I *HEAR* YOU *OUT* THERE IN *DEEP SPACE.* I HEAR YOUR CHILDREN *BUZZING* LIKE *FLIES.* YOU'RE HUNGRY.

MY FATHER SAID, "EVERYONE *DIES, WILLIAM.*"

THOMAS AND MARTHA WAYNE

SPACE SECTOR 666.

HE SAID, "*DEATH* IS THE *ONLY* THING YOU CAN *COUNT ON* IN THIS UNIVERSE."

YES.

I *KILLED* HIM TO PROVE HIS *POINT.*

I AM HUNGRY.

DEATH *COMPELS* US BECAUSE *POWERFUL* OR *WEAK, LOVED* OR *HATED*--

--NO ONE ESCAPES DEATH.

THAT INCLUDES *YOU.*

YEARS AGO, THE DAY EVERYONE THOUGHT *SUPERMAN* DIED WAS DECLARED A NATIONAL DAY OF MOURNING.

SINCE HE RETURNED, IT'S BECOME A DAY TO HONOR THE *SUPER-BEINGS* WHO GAVE THEIR *LIVES* PROTECTING THE WORLD--

--AND THE *INNOCENTS* WE FAILED TO SAVE.

AMONG THOSE INNOCENTS-- THE *SEVEN MILLION* WHO WERE INCINERATED WHEN *MONGUL* AND THE *CYBORG-SUPERMAN* DESTROYED COAST CITY.

PEOPLE ARGUED OVER WHAT TO DO WITH THE LAND. SOME WANTED TO LEAVE IT A *GRAVEYARD.* OTHERS A *MEMORIAL.*

THEY SAID WE'D NEVER COME BACK.

THEY SAID OUR CITY WOULD *STAY* DEAD.

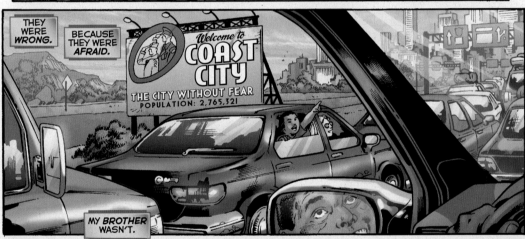

THEY WERE *WRONG.*

BECAUSE THEY WERE *AFRAID.*

Welcome to **COAST CITY**
THE CITY WITHOUT FEAR
POPULATION: 2,765,321

MY *BROTHER* WASN'T.

HIS *FAMILY* WASN'T.

DADDY! MOMMY! IT'S UNCLE H--

HE'S GOT A *SECRET IDENTITY,* JANE! *DON'T* SAY IT!

I *WASN'T* GONNA!

AND NEITHER WERE THE PEOPLE WHO FOLLOWED THEM HERE.

COAST CITY GOT A SECOND CHANCE.

--AND ARTIST AND CORPS CONSCIENCE *KYLE RAYNER*.

JOHN KNOWS THAT WHEN YOU'RE IN THE MILITARY, DEATH IS PART OF THE JOB.

GUY AND KYLE KNOW WHEN YOU'RE IN THE GREEN LANTERN CORPS, DEATH IS THE ONLY RETIREMENT.

AND WE ALL KNOW WHEN YOU'RE PART OF THE CAPED COMMUNITY, DEATH OPENS YOUR FRONT DOOR--

--AND WALKS RIGHT IN.

MY FATHER.

ABIN SUR.

COAST CITY.

YOU NEVER *LEARN* TO *LIVE* WITH IT.

IT JUST BECOMES A *PART* OF *WHO* YOU ARE.

BWOOOSH

YOUR ONLY CHOICE: KEEP PLAYING OR FOLD.

NO FEAR

I *NEVER* FOLD.

KATMA TUI.

JOHN MET HER WHEN SHE WAS STILL *OVERCOMPENSATING* FOR INHERITING SINESTRO'S RING--

--AND JOHN WAS STILL *OVERCOMPENSATING* FOR INHERITING *MINE.*

YOUR AIM IS ON, BUT YOUR CONSTRUCTS ARE TOO *COMPLICATED.* YOU'RE *OVER-THINKING.*

I'M *DOING* WHAT THE *LAST GUY DIDN'T.*

THE SHADOWS THEY WERE IN BROUGHT THEM TOGETHER. AND THEY FOUND WHAT CAROL AND I NEVER SEEMED TO--

--*COMMITMENT.* NOT TO AN *AIRCRAFT COMPANY* OR AN *INTERGALACTIC POLICE FORCE,* BUT TO *EACH OTHER.*

KATMA TUI DIED AT THE HANDS OF A *STAR SAPPHIRE.*

MONTHS LATER, JOHN WOULD MAKE A *MISTAKE* TRYING TO PREVENT THE *DESTRUCTION* OF A PLANET.

KYLE'S GIRLFRIEND, *ALEX,* WAS *MURDERED* BY A PSYCHOPATH NAMED *MAJOR FORCE* WHEN KYLE FIRST WORE THE RING.

HE FOUND HER *FOLDED* IN HIS REFRIGERATOR.

JADE WAS ANOTHER WOMAN KYLE LOVED.

THE DAUGHTER OF ALAN SCOTT. FOR A TIME, SHE WORE A RING.

SHE DIED IN SPACE SAVING A DOZEN SECTORS.

FACT IS, AFTER HIS ON-OFF GIRLFRIEND *ICE* RETURNED, GARDNER'S THE ONLY ONE OF US WHO'S HAD A *HAPPY ENDING.*

NONE OF US THOUGHT WE'D EVER BE *ENVIOUS* OF GUY GARDNER.

BUT HERE WE ARE.

HEROES.

LOOK HOW MANY PEOPLE **SHOWED**.

LOOK HOW MANY PEOPLE WE **LOST**.

I KNOW YOUR FATHER WASN'T A PART OF YOUR **LIFE** LIKE HE WAS **MINE**, DAMAGE, BUT CAN'T YOU AT LEAST **PRETEND** TO GIVE A DAMN?

CAN'T YOU AT LEAST **FACE** HIM?

I'M NOT TURNING MY **BACK** ON MY FATHER, ATOM SMASHER.

I'M LOOKING AT THE **FREEDOM FIGHTERS**. THE SECRET SOCIETY **MURDERED** THEM WHEN I WAS ON THEIR TEAM. I **WATCHED** THEM **DIE**. I **HEARD** THEM **DIE**.

I WAS LEFT **ALIVE** WITH A **CRUSHED** NASAL CAVITY AND A **MANGLED** PROFILE.

YOU WANT ME TO **FACE** MY **FATHER**, ATOM SMASHER?

HELL.

I CAN'T FACE **ANYONE**.

LEGENDS.

GOTHAM CITY.

BRUCE?

OH, NO!

I'VE MADE A TERRIBLE MISTAKE.

THOMAS AND MARTHA WAYNE

DICK GRAYSON UNCOVERED A *BODY SNATCHING* OPERATION THAT WAS *HARVESTING* SUPERHUMAN PARTS FOR *RE-USE.*

YOU'RE *SERIOUS?*

THIS IS AN *EXAMPLE* OF THE KIND OF *SICK* AND *TWISTED* THINGS WE'VE HAD TO DEAL WITH SINCE YOU WERE *LOST* TO THE *SPEED FORCE,* BARRY.

THE *GUILTY* HAVE GOTTEN *GUILTIER?* AND *BATMAN,* AQUAMAN AND THE *MARTIAN MANHUNTER* ARE *DEAD* BECAUSE OF IT?

SO WHO *ELSE?*

WHO ELSE *DIED* WHILE I WAS *GONE?*

I WANT TO *KNOW,* HAL.

OKAY.

ST. ROCH.
THE STONECHAT MUSEUM.

STONECHAT
MUSEUM
EST
1889

HOW THE *HELL* CAN YOU EVEN *ASK* ME THAT?

HOW CAN YOU EVEN *THINK* ABOUT IT, RAY?

I NEED A *FRIEND* TO COME WITH ME, CARTER. I CAN'T GO ALONE.

FORGET IT.

PLEASE, JUST...HOLD THE RECEIVER AWAY FROM YOUR EAR. I'M *COMING* THROUGH TO TALK *FACE-TO-FACE.*

NO, RAY.

YOU'RE *NOT.*

I TELL BARRY HOW RALPH BROKE DOWN AFTER SUE DIED.

HOW FELIX FAUST LED THE ELONGATED MAN TO HIS DEATH.

AND THE FASTEST MAN ALIVE DOES SOMETHING I HAVEN'T SEEN HIM DO SINCE HE'S BEEN *BACK*--

--HE *SITS* DOWN.

IRIS ALWAYS THOUGHT JEAN WAS A LITTLE *ODD*. SHE SEEMED TO *BRAG* A LOT, LIKE SHE HAD SOMETHING TO *PROVE*, BUT... *MURDERING* SUE?

IRIS AND SUE USED TO GET COFFEE WITH JEAN ONCE A MONTH.

THEY'D INVITE CAROL, BUT SHE WAS ALWAYS WORK--

CAROL? WHAT ABOUT--?

CAROL'S STILL RUNNING FERRIS AIR.

BUT WE HAVEN'T BEEN TOGETHER FOR A *LONG* TIME, BARRY.

IT'S *BETTER* THIS WAY.

"SHE'S SAFE."

HELLO? IS ANYONE THERE?

ALFRED?

RICHARD TRIED TO ARGUE WITH ME.

HE TOLD ME IT WASN'T SAFE, BUT I WANTED TO HONOR BRUCE'S WISHES. TO BE BURIED NEXT TO HIS PARENTS.

WHAT HAVE I DONE?

FLESH.

FLESH.

FLESH.

THEY TOOK BRUCE'S SKULL.

WHY WOULD SOMEONE TAKE BRUCE'S SKULL?

I THINK THE QUESTIONS WE SHOULD ANSWER FIRST ARE: WHO KNEW HE WAS BURIED HERE?

AND WHO KNEW BRUCE WAS BATMAN?

FLESH.

J'ONN J'ONZZ OF MARS.

KATMA TUI OF KORUGAR.

RONNIE RAYMOND OF EARTH.

FLESH.

FLESH.

FLESH.

KRETCHH!

WHERE ARE YOU GOING?

OUT.

AT LEAST CALL RAY *BACK.*

YOU'RE HIS *BEST* FRIEND!

KREEK

YOU'RE ALL HE *HAS* RIGHT NOW!

AND I GUESS RAY'S ALL *I* HAVE.

CARTER.

DAMMIT, WHY WON'T YOU PUT THE *WEAPONS* DOWN AND *TALK?*

RAGE.

WHY SHOULD *I TALK* TO YOU, KENDRA?

WHY ARE YOU EVEN *HERE?*

HIYA, WINGED WONDER.

YOU WANT TO KNOW WHAT HAWKGIRL WAS GOING TO *WHISPER* SO *SWEETLY* IN YOUR *EAR,* CARTER? ALL OF *US* KNEW IT.

RRAAHH!!

SHE *HATED* YOU.

PART TWO

RRRRNNGG

RRRRNNGG

RRRRNNGG

C'MON, CARTER.

VURRRRRRR

PICK UP.

...HELLO?

HELLO, RAY.

CARTER?

CARTER, PLEASE HEAR ME OUT BEFORE YOU HANG UP AGAIN.

I KNOW IT DOESN'T MAKE ANY SEMBLANCE OF *LOGIC*, BUT EVEN AFTER EVERYTHING JEAN DID I CAN'T STOP THINKING ABOUT HER.

AND WHEN I THINK OF HER, I THINK OF THIS GIRL, THIS BEAUTIFUL, SMART AND WITTY GIRL, THAT WAS *WAY* OUT OF MY LEAGUE SAYING "YES" AS I PROPOSED.

AFTER DEDICATING MY LIFE TO FIGURING OUT HOW THE UNIVERSE WORKS, FOR THAT ONE MOMENT, I THOUGHT I HAD. I THOUGHT I FOUND THE ANSWER TO *WHY* I WAS REALLY HERE.

HOW DID YOU LET KENDRA GO?

...CARTER?

COME ON OVER, RAY.

LET'S TALK.

I'LL BE RIGHT THERE.

THE SKY SEEMS SO MUCH DARKER TONIGHT.

I'M AFRAID TO TURN IT OFF.

THEN DON'T, DAD. LEAVE IT ON.

I'VE GOT THAT SAME AWFUL FEELING...

WHAT FEELING?

THE SAME FEELING I HAD WHEN BATGIRL DISAPPEARED. NO ONE KNEW EXACTLY WHAT HAD HAPPENED TO HER, BUT EVERYONE KNEW IT WAS *BAD.*

AND THERE WASN'T A DAMN THING I COULD DO ABOUT IT THEN EITHER.

WHEN I WAS IN PHYSICAL THERAPY, THERE WAS A SIGN ON THE GYM WALL. IT READ, "*NO MATTER HOW DARK THE NIGHT GETS, THE SUN STILL RISES IN THE MORNING.*"

EVERY DAY, I'D WAKE UP TWO HOURS BEFORE DAWN. BACK THEN IT'D TAKE ME THAT LONG TO GET INTO MY CHAIR, CLEAN UP AND GO OUTSIDE TO WATCH THE SUN RISE. BUT I DID IT. AND I STILL DO.

I LOVE LIFE, DAD. I LOVE EVERY SINGLE DAY.

I BROUGHT ENOUGH COFFEE TO LAST UNTIL SUNRISE.

YOU'RE AN AMAZING PERSON, YOU KNOW THAT?

LIKE FATHER, LIKE DAUGHTER.

I APPRECIATE THIS, MERA.

I AGREED TO THIS FOR *YOU*, GARTH--

--NOT *THEM.*

STILL. I KNOW THIS ISN'T EASY.

IF BRINGING ARTHUR'S REMAINS TO THE TOMBS OF ATLANTIS WILL EARN YOU THEIR ACCEPTANCE, IF THAT IS WHAT YOU TRULY WANT, I WILL SUPPORT IT.

IT'LL ALLOW ATLANTIS TO MOVE ON. AND I'LL LEAD THEM AS YOU AND ARTHUR WOULD HAVE. I'LL REDEDICATE OUR RESOURCES TOWARDS THE RECTIFICATION OF THE WORLD. BOTH LAND *AND* SEA.

ARTHUR WAS TRAPPED BETWEEN LAND AND SEA SINCE *BIRTH.* AND IT OFTEN GOT *VIOLENT.* DON'T UNDERESTIMATE THE CENTURIES OF RESENTMENT ATLANTIS HAS FOR THE SURFACE--

HE'S GONE.

ARTHUR?!

ARTHUR CURRY SON HUSBAND and FATHER

WHO WOULD DARE DESECRATE THE KING'S GRAVE?

OCEAN MASTER? OR BLACK MANTA?

MY ENEMIES CAN'T HURT ME ANYMORE, GARTH.

AQUAMAN?

MY KING?

FLESH.

FLESH.

HANK HALL OF EARTH.

RISE.

DON HALL OF EARTH.

RI--

DON HALL OF EARTH AT PEACE.

DON HALL OF EARTH.

RI--

DON HALL OF EARTH AT PEACE.

IN MEMORIAM
DONALD HALL
R.I.P.

DON HALL OF EARTH.

RI--

DON HALL OF EARTH AT PEACE.

SO IT'S SAME OLD, SAME OLD, *HUH*, BRO?

HAWK'S GOTTA DO *ALL* THE DIRTY WORK *HIMSELF.*

YOU'RE **NOT** AQUAMAN.

BECAUSE **YOU** SIT ON THE **THRONE** NOW, "AQUALAD"?

YOU'RE NO **KING**.

YOU TOOK **DOLPHIN** FROM ME, BUT YOU WON'T TAKE MY KINDGOM.

STAY BACK, MONSTER!

MERA?

I SHOULDN'T HAVE MENTIONED DOLPHIN.

I DIDN'T MEAN TO MAKE YOU **JEALOUS**.

THE SEA-WITCH SHOULDN'T BE, ARTHUR. AFTER **OUR** BRIEF AFFAIR--

THE EMPTY GRAVE OF BOSTON BRAND.

THIS IS ANOMALOUS.

YOU MEAN "BAD," RIGHT, STRANGER?

VERY.

I SENSE DEADMAN'S BODY IS NOW AS WANDERING AS HIS SPIRIT, YET THEY REMAIN UNDETECTABLE TO ME.

I SAW MORE OPEN GRAVES BACK THERE. WHAT'S GOING ON?

EVEN IF I WAS FULLY AWARE, ZATANNA, IT IS NOT MY PLACE TO SAY. I CANNOT DIRECTLY INTERFERE. I CAN ONLY GUIDE YOU.

SO GUIDE US TO SOMEONE WHO KNOWS WHAT THE HELL YOU'RE TALKING ABOUT.

YOU WERE THE ONES WHO ASKED US TO HIT THE TROUBLE ALERT FOR THE OTHER MAGIC FOLK SO WE CAN HOLD HANDS AND SING KUMBAYA YET AGAIN.

FOR ONCE, I'D LIKE TO UNDERSTAND WHY.

WORLDS HAVE DIED. WORLDS WILL RISE.

WHO THE HELL--?

YOU KNOW ME, BLUE DEVIL. ALL OF YOU DO.

FOR MY PAST SINS, I HAVE BEEN CURSED A PARIAH, DRAWN TO WORLDS TO WITNESS SUFFERING AND SLAUGHTER OF UNFATHOMABLE LEVELS.

EVEN IN DEATH, I CANNOT ESCAPE MY PENANCE. AND THIS TIME, NEITHER WILL YOU.

DON'T YOU WANT ME BACK, MERA?

I WANT YOU--

--OFF.

YOU DIDN'T HAVE HIS CHILD, TULA.

I WOULD HAVE.

BUT I DID. I AM WHAT ALL THE AQUAMEN LUST AFTER.

I'VE SEEN THE DEAD RETURN BEFORE. TRICKS. ILLUSIONS. MAGIC.

MY MAGIC--

--CAN STOP YOU.

KRRRNGGG

SIREN.

NO MORE SINGING.

YOU SAID AQUAGIRL AND AQUALAD WOULD BE TOGETHER FOREVER!

NKKK!

FWP FWP FWP

ARE YOU ANGRY WITH ME, MERA--

--OR YOURSELF?

FWP

TULA, IF IT IS YOU, AND I HOPE IT IS, FIGHT THIS DARK MYSTICISM --

YES, GARTH.

HOPE.

WELCOME BACK TO THE PEACE.

WELCOME TO THE BLACK LANTERN CORPS.

MERA, WE NEED YOU.

WE'LL SHARE.

OUR FAMILY IS HERE.

OUR SON CAN BE, TOO. YOU JUST HAVE TO COME BACK.

NNG.

MERA?!

MERA, DO YOU HEAR YOUR KING?!

MERAAAAAAAA!

YOUR THOUGHTS ARE MOVING *FASTER*, BARRY.

YOU'RE TRYING TO PREVENT ME FROM MANIPULATING THEM AGAIN.

THAT'S

THE

IDEA.

YOU CAN'T RUN AWAY FROM ME.

I'M NOT RUNNING AWAY.

HHFF!

AND I HAVEN'T BEEN MIXING AND MATCHING ALL THESE *CHEMICALS* FOR *FUN*.

DO YOU KNOW WHAT CARBON DISULFIDE, HEXANE AND METHANOL ALL HAVE IN *COMMON*?

I DO.

THEY'RE ALL *FLAMMABLE*.

FLASH FACT.

THE FLASH KEEPS THE FLAMES FROM SPREADING.

AND HE CREATES ONE HELL OF A *FURNACE*.

SORRY, J'ONN.

FIRE.

IT WAS J'ONN'S *KRYPTONITE*.

PART THREE

I CAN'T BELIEVE I DIDN'T NOTICE THIS BEFORE, FLASH, BUT YOU'RE A *LOT* LIKE PROFESSOR STEIN.

YOU'RE *BOTH* BORING OLD DUDES WHO KNOW ALL ABOUT CHEMICALS AND GIGAWATTS AND JUNK.

I *HATE* THINKING TOO HARD ABOUT STUFF THAT SUCKS, BUT RIGHT NOW I DON'T HAVE A CHOICE.

THERE'S A BIG *EMPTY* SPOT IN MY HEAD WHERE THE PROFESSOR USED TO HANG. I'VE GOT A *VACANCY* THAT NEEDS TO BE *FILLED*.

HOW ABOUT *YOU* BE MY NEW NERD BRAIN, FLASH?

THE RONNIE RAYMOND *I* KNEW MIGHT'VE MADE *LESS* THAN AVERAGE GRADES, BUT HE NEVER SAW PROFESSOR STEIN AS A *HUMAN DATABASE*.

HEY, I GOT A "*B*" IN P.E.

ONCE.

YOU WANT TO TRY AN EXPERIMENT, "*FIRESTORM*"?

LET'S SEE WHAT HAPPENS WHEN I TAKE THIS BLACK RING *OFF*.

RRARRR!!

POWER LEVELS 50.32%

HE WILL RISE, INVADER! AND THERE IS NOTHING YOU CAN DO TO STOP IT!

HAL! THE BLACK RINGS HAVE GROWN *ROOTS* INTO THEIR BODIES LIKE PLANTS.

WE'RE ALL CONNECTED, BARRY. INCLUDING YOU.

THEY RE-FORM IF THEY'RE DAMAGED. THEIR POWER LEVELS SOUND LIKE THEY'RE *INCREASING*.

ANY MORE IDEAS ON HOW TO *STOP* THEM?

NONE AT THE MOMENT NNGG!

RRAHH!

THEN I GUESS WE'RE ALL IN THE DARK.

NEW YORK CITY.

COLUMBIA UNIVERSITY.

GEN, I CAN'T GO TO THE MOVIES. I HAVE TO GET BACK TO STUDYING.

BUT YOU'VE BEEN STUDYING ALL NIGHT, JASON.

AND I STILL HAVE TO MEMORIZE THE CHEMICAL FORMULA FOR *FIRE RETARDANT.* WHAT IF THERE'S A HUGE INFERNO SOMEWHERE?

WHENEVER YOU OBSESS OVER YOUR FLASHCARDS THAT MEANS SOMETHING'S BOTHERING YOU.

IT'S *NOTHING.*

YOU BARELY SAID ANYTHING AT DINNER.

I DIDN'T FEEL LIKE TALKING.

CAN YOU TALK NOW? PLEASE?

GEN, I JUST STARTED COLLEGE. YOU'RE BARELY OUT OF HIGH SCHOOL. I'M NOT READY TO GET *ENGAGED.*

WHAT? BUT HOW DID--?

WHEN WE'RE SUPER-HEROING AROUND, OUR MINDS ARE LINKED. AND YOUR THOUGHTS ABOUT MARRIAGE AND A FAMILY ARE SO STRONG I CAN'T HELP BUT HEAR THEM.

IT'S JUST, I LIKE YOU SO MUCH, JASON. AND SINCE I MET YOU, EVERYTHING'S BEEN SO GREAT. IT'S HARD *NOT* TO THINK ABOUT OUR FUTURE.

AND I *WANT* ONE TOO. I DO.

BUT RIGHT NOW, I'M JUST TRYING TO GET THROUGH CHEMISTRY 201.

IF MY THOUGHTS ARE BOTHERING YOU...

...IF IT'S BETTER FOR US...

...MAYBE WE SHOULDN'T BE FIRESTORM ANYMORE.

VEET VEET VEET

WASHINGTON, D.C.
THE HEADQUARTERS OF THE JUSTICE LEAGUE OF AMERICA.

HELLO?!

HELLO? IS ANYONE HERE?

SOMEONE TURNED ON THE EMERGENCY SIGNAL, JASON.

WHO DO YOU THINK IT WAS?

THEY USED AQUAMAN'S CODE.

AQUAMAN'S DEAD.

THIS IS TOTALLY CREEPING ME OUT.

YEAH...

KAHNDAQ.

ON HEIGHTS.

OSCOW

I HAVE A NAME.

CO.

WASHINGTON D.C.

MY GOD! SOMETHING'S COME OUT OF THE TOMB OF THE UNKNOWNS! IT'S--

PLEASE-STA

PLEASE-STA

SKTT

JASON? WHAT WAS THAT?!

RAY? RAY, STAY WITH US.

YEAH! YOUR FRICTION LIGHTS THAT RIGHT UP!

LET'S SEE WHAT HAPPENS WHEN I TURN THE AIR AROUND YOU INTO GUN-POWDER.

WE'VE GOT TO REGROUP, HAL. LET ME ZIP US OUT OF HERE.

GET OUR BEARINGS. CLARK AND DIANA. WALLY AND JAY.

WE WERE NEVER REALLY TIGHT, WERE WE, HAL? DON'T THINK I DIDN'T CATCH YOU SCOPING OUT SUE WHEN SHE WAS WEARING A SKIRT.

AND YOU, RAY. YOU'RE NOT LOOKING ME IN THE EYES. WHAT'S WRONG?

YOU STILL FEEL BAD ABOUT WHAT JEAN DID TO MY LADY, DON'T YOU? WORSE YET--

COMPASSION.

--YOU STILL FEEL BAD FOR JEAN. SHE WAS A TERRIBLE PERSON, RAY. SHE LEFT YOU. SHE MURDERED MY WIFE.

IT WAS--NNN--AN ACCIDENT.

JEAN BROUGHT ALONG A FLAME-THROWER "JUST IN CASE." SHE KNEW WHAT SHE WAS DOING.

COMPASSION. IT'S SO HARD TO FIND IN THIS SOCIETY, ISN'T IT, BUN?

AHH--!

BUT A LITTLE BIT CAN GO SUCH A LONG WAY.

KLEK OCTA ROQ?

LEKORA LEK LEK.

WHAT'S SHE SAYING?

UNABLE TO TRANSLATE. LANGUAGE NOT RECOGNIZED.

WILL.

NOK.

CONNECTION SEVERED.

FLASH?

MERA? ARE YOU ALL RIGHT?

THOSE THINGS KILLED GARTH.

AQUALAD?!

THEY KILLED GARTH AND HE BECAME ONE OF THEM.

THEY DID THE SAME THING TO THE HAWKS.

RAY?

I CAN SENSE YOUR EMPATHY FOR OTHERS. YOU HAVE SPENT MUCH OF YOUR LIFE IN SUBATOMIC ISOLATION IN AN ATTEMPT TO UNLOCK THE SECRETS OF THE UNIVERSE FOR THE BENEFIT OF YOUR KIND.

OUR LIGHT DESIRES TO HEAL YOU.

YOU SPEAK ENGLISH?

WHEN WE WISH TO, GREEN LANTERN.

LORO KLEK. YES. THEY COLLECT A GREAT MANY POSSESSIONS.

WHO ARE THEY? THE PURPLE LANTERNS?

THE BEGINNING SEEMS NECESSARY.

THOUGH WE DISCARD NAMES AS WE DISCARD EVERYTHING ASSOCIATED WITH INDIVIDUALISM, YOU MAY CALL ME INDIGO-1.

I AM THE CHOSEN LEADER OF THE INDIGO TRIBE.

YOU WERE RIGHT, HAL. YOU'VE GOT A LOT TO CATCH ME UP ON.

WHERE DO I START--?

THE BEGINNING? IN THE BEGINNING THE UNIVERSE BELONGED TO THE DARKNESS--

--AND THEN THERE WAS LIGHT.

FOR SEVEN HUNDRED YEARS, THE UNIVERSE WAS NOTHING BUT BLINDING *WHITE LIGHT*.

THEN THE DARKNESS FOUGHT BACK AND THE WHITE LIGHT WAS SPLINTERED.

EVERY SENTIENT BEING BORN FROM THE LIGHT NOW CONTRIBUTES TO ITS EMOTIONAL SPECTRUM. OUR STATE OF BEING ADDS TO ITS RESPECTIVE LIGHT. AND IT CAN BE COLLECTED AND CONDENSED INTO POWER.

TODAY, THE *RED RAGE* ALL LIFE FEELS IS HARNESSED BY AN ANCIENT ENEMY OF THE GUARDIANS OF THE UNIVERSE-- *ATROCITUS* AND HIS PACK OF RED LANTERNS.

THE *ORANGE LIGHT* OF *AVARICE* HAS BEEN CLAIMED, LIKE THE LIVES OF THE ORANGE LANTERNS, BY THE OBSESSIVE AND GLUTTONOUS *LARFLEEZE.*

THE BLINDING *YELLOW TERROR* IS WIELDED BY THE RENEGADE GREEN LANTERN *SINESTRO* AND HIS SELF-NAMED CORPS.

THE BALANCE OF THE SPECTRUM AND THE ESSENTIAL LIGHT TO DESTROYING THE BLACK LANTERNS SHINES IN THE HANDS OF THE *GREEN LANTERN CORPS.*

THE GLOW OF *BLUE HOPE* IS ON THE VERGE OF EXTINCTION, KEPT ALIVE ONLY BY THE UNDYING FAITH OF *SAINT WALKER* AND A HANDFUL OF OTHERS.

AND THE *VIOLET* THROES OF LOVE EMPOWER THE *STAR SAPPHIRES*, WHO ATTEMPT TO CONVERT ALL TO THEIR WAY OF BEING.

SO THE DEAD ARE INVADING THE CORPS HOMEWORLDS...BUT *WHY* ARE THEY INVADING EARTH?

I BELIEVE IT IS BECAUSE YOU AND YOUR KIND HAVE HALTED ENDLESS THREATS AGAINST THE UNIVERSE.

YOU *CAN HEAR ME?*

AND THE BLACK LANTERNS ARE NOT THE INVADERS IN THIS WAR. *WE* ARE THE INVADERS. WE ARE THE TRESPASSERS. BUT WE BRING *GOODNESS.* WE BRING *LIFE.* IT IS A SHAME SO MANY DO NOT LIVE IT WELL.

THESE *BLACK LANTERNS* AREN'T REALLY THEM.

AREN'T REALLY *WHO?*

RALPH AND SUE. J'ONN AND RONNIE.

RONNIE RAYMOND? HE'S OUT THERE TOO?

BARRY'S RIGHT. WHEN RALPH WAS TURNED TO ASH, SUE HAD NO REACTION.

BUT THAT THING KNEW EVERYTHING ARTHUR DID. ALL THE PAIN HE ENDURED BECAUSE OF ATLANTIS.

MAYBE THE *DEAD* AREN'T WEARING THE *RINGS.* MAYBE THE *RINGS* ARE WEARING THE *DEAD.*

MAYBE THE RINGS ARE SOME SORT OF ADVANCED ORGANIC COMPUTER THAT DOWNLOAD THEIR MEMORIES BECOMING SOME SORT OF...OF *SIMULATOR* PROGRAM TO ATTACK US...

...BUT *WHY--?*

THEY FEED OFF EMOTION. THOSE THAT RISE DO SO TO ELICIT SUCH A RESPONSE.

BUT WE CAN STOP THEM. YOU DID. YOU CHANNELED HAL'S POWER RING.

GREEN LIGHT, REINFORCED WITH ANOTHER SUCH AS OURS, WILL NEUTRALIZE THE BLACK RINGS AND LEAVE THEM SUSCEPTIBLE TO CONVENTIONAL DAMAGE.

ONCE DESTROYED, THE RING INITIATES A FEEDBACK, WHICH RENDERS THE BLACK LANTERN INERT. THE MORE SHADES OF THE EMOTIONAL SPECTRUM SHINING TOGETHER, THE STRONGER THE LIGHT.

THAT IS WHY WE HAVE COME TO YOU, GREEN LANTERN. TOGETHER, THE SEVEN CORPS CAN REPLICATE THE WHITE LIGHT OF CREATION. TOGETHER WE WILL BE CAPABLE OF LOCATING AND DESTROYING THE SOURCE OF THE BLACK RINGS.

YOU HAVE PERSONAL CONNECTIONS TO THE MOST POWERFUL MEMBERS OF THE FIVE REMAINING CORPS. SUCH AS CAROL FERRIS.

CAROL? WHAT ABOUT CAROL?

SHE IS ONCE AGAIN THE STAR SAPPHIRE. SHE IS ON ZAMARON.

THEN WE'RE GOING TO ZAMARON *FIRST--*

HAL, HOLD *UP!*

IF WE *NEED* A GREEN LANTERN TO TAKE APART THESE BLACK ONES, WE NEED *YOU.* JOHN, GUY AND KYLE AREN'T HERE.

UNTIL THEN, FIND ALAN SCOTT. AND ANYONE ELSE WHO CAN WIELD LIGHT. THE RAY. HALO. MAYBE THEY CAN DO SOME DAMAGE.

WE NEED MORE THAN THAT. DEATH IS LITERALLY SWEEPING ACROSS THE EARTH.

DEATH IS OVERRATED.

HEY. MERA JUST WATCHED AQUAMAN ORCHESTRATE THE *MURDER* OF AQUALAD. RAY WAS NEARLY SKEWERED BY ONE OF MY WIFE'S BEST FRIENDS.

DON'T JUST TELL *ME* DEATH IS OVERRATED. TELL MERA. TELL RAY.

I DIDN'T MEAN IT LIKE THAT--

TELL YOUR FATHER. BARRY. DON'T GO THERE--

I HAVE TO GET THROUGH THAT THICK SKULL OF YOURS SOMEHOW.

WHAT AM I SUPPOSED TO *DO?* WHAT DO YOU *WANT* ME TO DO?

I WANT YOU TO HELP US GET EVERYONE WE CAN TOGETHER. HELP US WITH A PLAN OF ATTACK BEFORE YOU FLY OFF.

POWER RINGS-- GREEN OR YELLOW OR AQUA-BLUE--THIS IS *YOUR* ARENA.

I CAN'T BELIEVE AFTER EVERYTHING YOU'VE BEEN THROUGH, AFTER THE DESTRUCTION OF COAST CITY AND YOUR POSSESSION BY PARALLAX AND AFTER CLAWING YOUR WAY UP FROM THE ABSOLUTE *BOTTOM* TO GET YOUR LIFE BACK--

--YOU *HAVEN'T* CHANGED. YOU STILL FLY OFF HALF-COCKED. YOU STILL LIVE EVERY DAY LIKE IT'S YOUR *FIRST.*

AND SINCE *YOU'VE* GOTTEN BACK YOU'VE BEEN LIVING EVERY DAY LIKE IT'S YOUR *LAST.*

THE FASTEST MAN ALIVE WAS ALWAYS *LATE* BECAUSE HE STOPPED AND BEFRIENDED THE PEOPLE HE SAVED. HE SPENT HOURS METICULOUSLY ANALYZING A CRIME SCENE SO HE COULD FIND JUSTICE FOR A VICTIM THAT DIDN'T HAVE ANY.

HE SLOWED DOWN AND REJOINED THE *REST* OF US EVERY CHANCE HE GOT.

YOU'RE *RUNNING* NONSTOP BECAUSE YOU'RE *AFRAID* IT'LL BE TAKEN AWAY AGAIN.

YOU'RE RIGHT, HAL. I *AM* AFRAID TO LOSE IT AGAIN.

BUT I LEARNED THE *HARD* WAY, AFTER EVERYTHING THE REVERSE-FLASH DID WHEN HE BROUGHT ME BACK, I NEED TO SLOW DOWN. FOR MYSELF. MY FAMILY AND FRIENDS. IRIS. WALLY. YOU.

I MISSED A LOT OF GOOD TIMES WE COULD'VE SHARED WHILE I WAS AWAY. AND A LOT OF BAD TIMES WE COULD'VE HELPED EACH OTHER THROUGH.

THIS IS ONE OF THEM, HAL. *THIS* IS WHY I'M BACK.

LET'S *BOTH* SLOW DOWN AND FIGURE OUT A *PLAN.*

YOU'RE RIGHT, BARRY. I'M--

WE'RE BAAAAAAACK!

NOK NEK NEK KLEK?

NOK. WE MUST GO.

HEY! WAIT A SECOND--

ONE WALL OF HYDROCHLORIC ACID, COMING UP!

YEAH. YOU *LOVED* HER, NERD. ...OH, YOU'RE ANGRY NOW, JASON? GO AHEAD AND YELL. I'LL TAKE THAT TOO. YEAH. I'LL BURN THROUGH *EVERYTHING* YOU'VE GOT 'TIL THERE'S *NOTHING* LEFT.

POWER LEVELS 56.57%

POWER LEVELS 56.58%

POWER LEVELS 56.59%

MAN, YOU'RE LIKE A NEVER-ENDING BATTERY. THIS *RULES*.

JOHN MONROE OF EARTH.

ARTHUR LIGHT OF EARTH.

MAXWELL LORD OF EARTH.

CRYSTAL FROST OF EARTH.

JOHN RAVENHAIR OF EARTH.

ALEXANDER LUTHOR OF EARTH-3.

RISE.

PART FOUR

"DO YOU THINK BECAUSE SUPERMAN AND THE FLASH AND GREEN ARROW CHEATED DEATH BEFORE, THEY CAN CHEAT IT AGAIN?"

COAST CITY.

THEY CANNOT ESCAPE MY LORD. THEY *WILL* NOT.

POWER LEVELS 93.55%

"LET THERE BE LIGHT" SPARKED THE BEGINNING OF THE WAR.

OUR BLACKEST NIGHT WILL END IT.

MARTIN JORDAN

JESSICA JORDAN

"AND EVEN THE BRIGHTEST OF LIGHTS WILL BE BLOWN OUT."

THE INDIGO LANTERNS CLAIMED WE WOULD ONLY BE CAPABLE OF NEUTRALIZING THE BLACK RINGS WITH A GREEN LANTERN. AND YET THEY TELEPORT HAL JORDAN AWAY?

I GUESS THEY PRIORITIZED, MERA. FROM WHAT INDIGO-1 SAID, THEY NEED HAL TO RALLY TOGETHER THE OTHER CORPS, LOCATE THE SOURCE OF THE BLACK RINGS--

--AND PULL THE PLUG.

WHICH MEANS OUR JOB IS TO HOLD THE FORT UNTIL THE LITE-BRITE BRIGADE DO THEIR THING. THE FORT BEING EARTH.

WE NEED TO GET CLEAR OF HERE AND MAKE SURE EVERYONE'S UP TO SPEED.

WHERE'S FIRESTORM?

FLASH!!

DON'T GO *RUNNING* AWAY YET!

WITH JASON ON BOARD, I CAN TRANSMUTE *ORGANICS*--!

POWER LEVELS 93.88%

WILLPOWER NOW, JASON? *PFFT.* IT'S USELESS BANGING HEADS WITH ME, BUT I'LL TAKE IT. NOW WHERE *WERE* WE, FLASH? I THINK I WAS ABOUT TO TAKE YOUR *"BRAAA!!!!NS!"* BUT I JUST GOT A *NEW* ONE, SO GIVE ME YOUR HEART--

--HEART-- HEART-- *HEART*--

MERA. WHAT HAVE YOU BEEN DOING BEHIND MY BACK?

ARTHUR-- STAY HERE.

I DON'T STAY.

JUST KEEP THEM BACK, BARRY --

--FOR THREE MORE SECONDS.

TAKE A DEEP BREATH AND HOLD ON TIGHT. I'VE BEEN TINKERING WITH MY SIZE-CONTROLLING BELT, BUT I HAVEN'T DONE THIS BEFORE.

DONE WHAT?

9-1-1. WHAT'S YOUR EMERGENCY?

HELLO? HELLO? IF YOU CAN'T TALK--

GOTHAM CITY.

LISTEN TO THOSE SCREAMS OF HORROR.

I WANT TO FEEL IT TOO.

FEAR.

...NOT JUST THEM RISING ANYMORE, IT'S US TOO. I GOT VERIFICATION FROM THE CHEETAH THAT THE FORMERLY DECEASED DOCTOR POLARIS JUST RIPPED THE HEART OUT OF THE NEW ONE.

THE NEW WHO?

SECURITY LEVEL SIX ACTIVATED.

JOHN NICHOL. THE NEW DOCTOR POLARIS. HE WAS A MEMBER OF OUR SOCIETY AND MY CHIEF SOURCE OF INTEL ON THE BLUE BEETLE.

A TRAGIC LOSS, I'M SURE.

IT WAS FOR BUSINESS, LUTHOR.

MR. LUTHOR, CALCULATOR. I'M TIRED OF YOU PEOPLE GETTING TOO COMFORTABLE WITH ME. ANOTHER EXAMPLE: YOUR INVADING ONE OF MY PERSONAL LABS WITH THIS CALL. NO ONE HAS THIS NUMBER.

ENTRIES FOUR, FIVE AND SIX SEALED.

I GET PAID BECAUSE I HAVE ALL THE NUMBERS. EVEN YOURS.

DO YOU KNOW HOW MANY PEOPLE I'VE KILLED OVER THE YEARS? IF THE DEAD ARE RISING, I'LL HAVE MY OWN PROBLEMS. AND TO BE THOROUGHLY HONEST, I'M SICK OF YOU AND THE REST OF THOSE DELUSIONAL SCABS HUGGING THE EDGES OF MY GREATNESS AS IF SOMEHOW WE WERE ALL ON THE "SAME TEAM."

WE'RE NOT.

KSSSHHH

KLANK

SUB-LAB NINETEEN SECURE.

AS FAR AS I'M CONCERNED--

--IT'S EVERY MAN FOR HIMSELF.

DECEASED

"ONLY THE DEAD WITH EMOTIONAL TIES TO PEOPLE LIKE US ARE RISING. THE REST ARE STAYING IN THEIR GRAVES."

"POINT ME TO ALAN SCOTT."

THIS IS THE FLASH.

IF YOU'RE RECEIVING THIS, CHANCES ARE YOU ALREADY KNOW WHAT WE'RE UP AGAINST.

BLACK RINGS HAVE DESCENDED ON EARTH AND ARE RAISING OUR FRIENDS, FAMILY AND ENEMIES FROM THE DEAD--

BUT THESE BLACK LANTERNS ARE NOT THEM.

AND THEY ARE NOT UNSTOPPABLE.

GREEN LANTERN AND HIS CORPS HAVE SET OUT TO DESTROY THE SOURCE BEHIND THESE BLACK RINGS.

THAT LEAVES US HERE TO PROTECT EARTH UNTIL HE DOES.

THESE THINGS ARE ATTRACTED TO ALL KINDS OF EMOTIONAL OUTBURSTS POSITIVE AND NEGATIVE. SO FIRST THINGS FIRST, KEEP YOUR EMOTIONS IN CHECK.

THAT MEANS YOU, ARROW.

SECONDLY, WHEN EXPOSED TO INTENSE LIGHT, THEIR BLACK RINGS BECOME VULNERABLE. TRICK IS: THAT USUALLY INCLUDES THE POWER FROM A GREEN LANTERN'S RING. BUT SOME OF YOU OUT THERE MIGHT BE ABLE TO WEAKEN THE RINGS ENOUGH WITH YOUR OWN LIGHT TO DESTROY THEM.

"WE'RE ASKING ALL OF YOU *ABLE* TO SHINE--DO IT AS *BRIGHTLY* AS YOU CAN."

COAST CITY.

LIGHT IS EVERYTHING TO THEM.

POWER LEVELS 97.77%

ESPECIALLY IN THE END.

BUT THE TUNNEL OF LIGHT THEY SEE? IT LEADS TO WHERE THEY LEAST EXPECT: THE GUARDIANS' ULTIMATE *LIE.*

IT'S HIDDEN HERE, BENEATH THE *DEAD.*

POWER LEVELS 97.79%

BARRY?

WALLY?

GOT YOUR MESSAGE AND SPREADING THE WORD.

TITANS ARE READY TO FIGHT TOO, FLASHS. WHERE SHOULD WE GO?

"WHEREVER THERE'S *TROUBLE,* BART."

MY RING DOESN'T EXACTLY OPERATE LIKE HAL'S, ATOM. IT'S NOT CONNECTED TO THAT BATTERY OUT THERE ON OA. IT'S ITS OWN POWER SOURCE.

BUT HERE GOES NOTHING.

YEAH, ALAN. *"NOTHING."*

IT'S KEEPING THEM *BACK,* BUT FOR HOW LONG? AND WHAT CAN THE *REST* OF US DO?

PLENTY.

WNKH WNKH

WATER? WHAT'S SHE GONNA DO? *DROWN* THEM?

YOU CAN'T FEEL FEAR, DAMAGE. THAT'S JUST WHAT THEY WANT.

I'M *NOT* AFRAID, ATOM. I WAS POINTING OUT THE *ABSURDITY* OF TRYING TO SUFFOCATE THE DEAD.

MEANING YOU'RE COVERING UP FEAR WITH ATTITUDE.

WHY ARE YOU HANGING ON MY SHOULDER?

YOU'RE *AL PRATT'S* BOY.

THOUGH TO TELL YOU THE TRUTH, I WASN'T THAT AWARE OF YOUR FATHER UNTIL *AFTER* I TOOK THE NAME.

I DON'T WEAR THIS MASK FOR THE ATOM. I WEAR IT SO I *REMEMBER* NOT TO PULL MY PUNCHES LIKE THE REST OF YOU.

BECAUSE YOU'RE SCARED.

WELL, AFTER ALL OF *THIS*, WHO THE HELL *WOULDN'T* BE?!

AL?

DON'T LISTEN TO THE LITTLE MAN, SON.

RAGE.

FEAR.

LOVE.

YOU'RE *ANGRY* WITH ME, AREN'T YOU? ALL THOSE YEARS AND I NEVER EVEN BOTHERED TO PLAY A GAME OF *CATCH*.

MY DAD NEVER KNEW ABOUT ME.

OF COURSE I DID. I JUST DIDN'T *WANT* YOU.

YOU'RE TRYING TO DETONATE YOUR FISTS THE SAME WAY I USED TO, BUT I CAN *ABSORB* YOUR POWER, SON. AND IF I CAN'T GET AT YOUR HEART THE *EASY* WAY-- --I'LL JUST BLOW YOU APART AND PICK THROUGH THE PIECES.

NOT IF I RESTRAIN YOUR "ATOMIC-PUNCH" WITH A LITTLE CREATIVE MOLECULAR JUGGLING.

NOW STAY THE HELL AWAY FROM HIM!

I DON'T KNOW WHAT TO DO.

I DO. WE DO THIS *YOUR* WAY, GRANT. WE BEAT THEM DOWN *AGAIN* AND *AGAIN* UNTIL IT'S OVER.

NOT FOR YOUR FATHER, BUT FOR THE REST OF THE WORLD. THINK YOU CAN HANDLE THAT?

HELL, YEAH.

HOPE.

GRANT!

POWER LEVELS 100%

MY SWEET, SWEET RAY.

JEAN?

THIS WILL BE *TWICE* I'VE TURNED YOUR LITTLE WORLD INSIDE OUT.

POWER LEVELS 100%

WHAT... ...WHAT *IS* THAT?

Welcome to COAST CITY

"THAT *VOICE*."

SPACE SECTOR 666.

THE PLANET RYUT.

POWER LEVELS 100%

THE LIGHT AWAITS.

WALLY. BART.

CHANGE OF PLANS. TELL EVERYONE TO GET TO COAST CITY *PRONTO*.

I FEEL... SOMETHING--

TRANSPORTING.

SPACE SECTOR 2814.

--BLACK HAND--?

PART FIVE

THE BLACKEST NIGHT WILL DESCEND UPON US ALL. WITHOUT PREJUDICE OR MERCY. WITHOUT REASON. THE SEVEN CORPS WILL FALL. AS WILL THE UNIVERSE. BACK TO A PLACE DEVOID OF LIGHT. OF EMOTION. OF LIFE.
THE BOOK OF OA: COSMIC REVELATIONS, VERSE 3

SPACE SECTOR 666.
RYUT.

LIKE THE REST OF THE SELF-APPOINTED GUARDIANS, GANTHET AND SAYD WERE BORN ON THE PLANET MALTUS. THE WORLD WHERE *LIFE* FIRST BEGAN.

THAT GAVE THEM THE VALIDATION TO ACT AS THE ULTIMATE AUTHORITY FIGURES ON INTERGALACTIC ORDER.

THAT DOESN'T MEAN THEY'VE HANDLED IT ALL THAT WELL.

THE BLACK LANTERN IS NOT HERE.

"THE BLACK LANTERN IS NOT HERE." A *REMARKABLY* ASTUTE OBSERVATION, GANTHET.

OVER THE LAST YEAR, THE OTHER CORPS HAVE BEEN AT WAR.

BUT TODAY, FRIENDS, ENEMIES AND EX-GIRLFRIENDS HAVE TO STAND UNITED.

THIS HOLE IS EMPTY. THERE'S *NOTHING* WORSE THAN *EMPTY.*

HIP HIP HOORAY.

WHERE IS THE BLACK BATTERY, GUARDIAN SLIME?!

SAY IT, RED, DON'T SPRAY IT.

I SENSE THE GUARDIAN WHO BETRAYED US IS WITHIN THE BLACK LANTERN'S PRESENCE.

WE CAN TAKE US TO HER. AND TOGETHER WE CAN DESTROY THE DARKNESS BEHIND THIS.

THEN LET'S ALL SHUT UP--

--AND LIGHT UP.

WALLY! GRANDPA!

CALL ME BARRY OR FLASH, BART. "GRANDPA" MAKES ME FEEL OLD.

I'M YOUR GRANDSON FROM THE 31ST CENTURY. YOU *ARE* OLD.

SO I'VE GOT *GOOD NEWS* AND I'VE GOT *BAD NEWS*. WHAT DO YOU WANT FIRST?

THE *GOOD* NEWS.

THE *BAD* NEWS.

SORRY, WALLY. SENIORITY WINS.

GOOD NEWS IS: NO ONE'S REALLY SURE *HOW* OR *WHY*, BUT WHEN THE BLACK LANTERNS TRY TO TAKE DOVE'S HEART--

DOVE? OF HAWK AND DOVE? I THOUGHT THEY WERE BOTH DEAD.

THERE'S A *NEW* DOVE, BARRY. A *GIRL*.

WHEN THE BLACK LANTERNS TRY TO TAKE DOVE'S HEART, SHE LIGHTS UP LIKE A *ROMAN CANDLE* AND BURNS THEM UP. AND THEY *DON'T* COME BACK.

AAAAAIIII IIIIEEEEEE

SO SOMEHOW DOVE'S TAPPING INTO THE WHITE LIGHT THE LANTERNS WERE TALKING ABOUT. LET'S GET HER FRONT-AND-CENTER.

THE TITANS ARE ALREADY WORKING ON THAT...

CONNECTION SEVERED.

"...WHICH LEADS ME TO THE *BAD NEWS.*"

"DONNA TROY WAS BITTEN BY A BLACK LANTERN. AND SHE STARTED GETTING SICK."

"THE GUARDIANS OF OA."

WE MIGHT NOT HAVE GREEN LANTERNS TO HELP, BUT WE'VE GOT ONE STEP BETTER IF YOU'RE TALKING SHEER POWER.

DON'T STOP RUNNING, BART. AND DON'T FOCUS ON HIM. FOCUS ON THE ALIENS FLOATING IN THE SKY.

WHO?

WE GET THEM CLEAR OF THIS BLACK GOO AND MAYBE THEY'LL WAKE UP AND LEND US A HAND--

YOU SHOULD'VE TAKEN HER TO DOCTOR MID-NITE OR S.T.A.R. LABS.

WE TRIED, WALLY. BUT DONNA SAID IF SHE WAS GOING DOWN, SHE WAS GOING DOWN *FIGHTING*--

--UM, *WHERE* ARE WE GOING? IS *THAT* THE BLACK LANTERN *BOSS?*

FLSSH

FLSSH

BARRY ALLEN OF EARTH.

PART SIX

--I'VE ALREADY TRIGGERED THE PROCESS.

SCANNING FOR RAGE.

SCANNING FOR HOPE.

SCANNING FOR LOVE.

SCANNING FOR AVARICE.

SCANNING FOR FEAR.

SCANNING FOR COMPASSION.

YUH-OH.

SENTIENT LOCATED.

BARRY ALLEN OF EARTH.

YOU HAVE THE ABILITY TO INSTILL GREAT HOPE.

OH, NO! NO, YOU DON'T!! GET BACK **HERE!**

"I DON'T SHARE WITH ANYONE!"

GIVE ME ALL OF YOUR RINGS!!

IT'LL BE MINE!

PRETTY RED RING.

AAAAAIIIEEEEEEEE

WHEN NEKRON STRIKES THE ENTITY... W-WE *SHARE* THE PAIN.

BECAUSE WE ARE *ALL* CONNECTED. WE ARE ALL *ALIVE*. EVERY LIVING THING IN THE UNIVERSE IS *DYING*.

WHY ISN'T IT FIGHTING BACK?

THAT'S IT, BARRY. *THE ENTITY*. IT'S LIKE PARALLAX AND ION. A *LIVING POWER*. AND NEKRON DUG IT UP FOR US.

IT JUST NEEDS A *PILOT*.

NO!

YOU HAD YOUR CHANCE WITH PARALLAX!

THIS IS MY DUTY!

THIS IS WHY I AM ALIVE!

I AM ALIVE TO LEAD US OUT OF THE BLACKEST NIGHT!

I DEMAND YOUR POWER, ENTITY!

AND I WILL FINALLY PROVE TO THE UNIVERSE...

THAAL SINESTRO, OF KORUGAR.

PART EIGHT

THE TRUTH IS, I AM AFRAID OF ONE THING.

I'M AFRAID TO GET CLOSE TO PEOPLE.

BECAUSE BLACK HAND IS RIGHT.

EVENTUALLY, EVERYONE WILL DIE.

A POET ONCE SAID, "CARPE DIEM QUAM MINIMUM CREDULA POSTERO" WHICH MEANT, "SEIZE THE DAY, TRUSTING AS LITTLE AS POSSIBLE IN THE FUTURE."

MOST PEOPLE ONLY KNOW THE FIRST PART-- "CARPE DIEM"--PROBABLY BECAUSE NOT TRUSTING TOMORROW IS TOO DAMN CYNICAL. IT IS TO ME, ANYWAY.

SURE YOU CAN'T RELY ON TOMORROW, WE'RE NOT GUARANTEED WE'LL HAVE IT--

OH, MY GOD.

ARTHUR?

BABUM

LOVE.

MERA--?

RAGE COMPROMISED.

SHINK!

SHINK!

ARRGHH!

MERA?!

HAL? WHAT'S GOING ON?

WHAT'S HAPPENING TO MERA?

SHE'S GOING INTO CARDIAC ARREST.

WHY?

HER HEART HAS STOPPED. GIVE ME YOUR HAND, AQUAMAN.

LOVE.

YOUR HEART IS BEATING AGAIN AND IT WILL HELP HERS BEAT AGAIN TOO.

WHILE MY BLUE LIGHT *REVERSES* THE EFFECTS OF THE RED RING.

KFFFF!

ARTHUR?

ARE WE DEAD?

NO.

HAWK, PLEASE, CALM DOWN. THEY ONLY WANT TO HELP.

THEY *TOUCH* ME *AGAIN* THEY LOSE A *FINGER*.

I WANT TO KNOW WHAT'S GOING ON, *DOVE.* I WANT TO KNOW WHAT THE HELL'S HAPPENING RIGHT *NOW!*

MAXWELL LORD.

I DON'T KNOW WHY *YOU'RE* HERE, BUT DON'T THINK YOU CAN--

ARE...ARE YOU ALL RIGHT, SIR?

I'M FINE.

KYLE?!

RALPH?

SUE?

BARRY.

THEY'RE NOT HERE.

WHY?

OH, NO.

HE'S FROM *YOUR* WORLD. DISPOSE OF THIS HAIRLESS THIEF!

YOU *DO* REALIZE WHAT YOU'VE JUST DONE, DON'T YOU, LARFLEEZE?

WHAT? WHAT'S SO FUNNY?

YOU FINALLY *GAVE* SOMEONE SOMETHING, YOU RIDICULOUS RODENT.

HEE!

I DIDN'T... YOU...

...I HELPED SAVE EVERYONE! I DEMAND WHAT I WAS PROMISED!

YOU BELONG TO ME, BLUE ONE!

SAYD--

IT IS ALL RIGHT, GANTHET. PERHAPS I CAN HELP HIM.

BUT THE CORPS--

THERE IS MUCH TO DISCUSS ABOUT THE FUTURE OF THE CORPS.

OF *ALL* THE CORPS.

THE ANTI-MONITOR HAS RETURNED, BUT OUR IMMEDIATE CONCERN SHOULD BE WITH *BLACK HAND.* HE IS *MISSING.*

SO IS INDIGO-1. AND HER TRIBE.

"WHERE DID THEY GO?"

MORAT ABIN SUR LOK WOR WOR. KRONA RAMP LEK LARFLEEZE ET DOOME.

NOK.

NOK.

NOK.

GOTHAM CITY.

"I DON'T KNOW WHY THE EARTH OR THE SKY OR PEOPLE EXIST. AND THE FACT IS, I'LL PROBABLY NEVER KNOW."

BUT I DO KNOW *ONE* THING, BARRY. WHEN YOU TOLD BLACK HAND *WE* WERE THE ONES THAT GIVE *LIFE* PURPOSE, YOU WERE RIGHT.

WE ALL LIVE FOR DIFFERENT REASONS, HAL. IT'S UP TO US TO FIGURE THOSE OUT.

I JUST WISH WE KNEW WHY THE WHITE LIGHT RESURRECTED AQUAMAN AND THE OTHERS, BUT NOT EVERYONE.

GANTHET THINKS THERE'S A BIGGER PICTURE TO IT ALL. ONE WE'LL EVENTUALLY SEE...

...I DON'T KNOW.

DO YOU THINK WITHOUT NEKRON PULLING THE STRINGS, THE RESURRECTIONS ARE OVER?

I THINK *DEAD* IS *DEAD* FROM HERE ON OUT--

THOMAS AND MARTHA WAYNE

--EXCEPT FOR HIM. THAT BLACK LANTERN BATMAN DIDN'T RECOGNIZE ANY OF US. IT WASN'T BRUCE.

TIM DRAKE IS RIGHT. BRUCE IS *ALIVE.*

WHAT ABOUT THE ENTITY? THE WHITE LIGHT?

DID IT DISAPPEAR BACK INTO THE EARTH? IS IT INSIDE BLACK HAND?

NO. I CAN FEEL IT *OUT* THERE, BARRY. URGING US TO BREAK AWAY FROM THE PAST AND THE *BLACKEST NIGHT...*

"...AND HEAD INTO TOMORROW."

BLACKEST NIGHT
VARIANT COVER GALLERY

BLACKEST NIGHT 1A
by Ethan Van Sciver with Hi-Fi

BLACKEST NIGHT 3
by Ethan Van Sciver with Hi-Fi

BLACKEST NIGHT 6
by Rodolfo Migliari

BLACKEST NIGHT DIRECTOR'S COMMENTARY

The creative team and the editors look back on their favorite moments from BLACKEST NIGHT.

GEOFF JOHNS/Writer IVAN REIS/Penciller OCLAIR ALBERT/Inker JOE PRADO/Inker

ALEX SINCLAIR/Colorist NICK J. NAPOLITANO/Letterer ADAM SCHLAGMAN/Associate Editor EDDIE BERGANZA/Editor

ISSUE #1

GEOFF: Ok, now, let's get into it.

PAGE 2/panel 1

ALEX: Still one of my favorite panels from the entire series. Thanks to this panel, I knew just how cool and how HARD it was going to be working on BLACKEST NIGHT.

PAGE 2/panel 2

EDDIE: You pretty much knew the tone of the book, when on the second page you had Black Hand licking the skull. It really would be like no DC series before it.

PAGE 4-5

ALEX: Here was the first of many Guy Gardner ring fixes.

IVAN: I started to do a different symbol for the GLs... now they have a 3-D symbol on their chests... and not a simple drawing... I'm not talking about the energy symbol.

PAGE 6/panel 4

ADAM: Heroes Day doesn't just honor super-heroes, but REAL heroes like firemen, cops and soldiers.

PAGE 6/panel 5

GEOFF: The entire thematic concept of Green Lantern, for me, is overcoming fear. In the original comics back in the '60s, Hal was chosen because he was without fear, but for me, really, the emotional reality is that he's able to overcome fear. No one is without fear unless they're crazy. We just work through it. So "NO FEAR" means a lot more than just leaping before looking…though Hal does plenty of that, too.

Diane Nelson, the new President of DC Entertainment, uses "NO FEAR" as the model for the company. Ironically, GREEN LANTERN is the first film DC Entertainment is fully involved in, which is going to be AWESOME!

IVAN: "Fear" is the key word to all GL mythology

PAGE 9/panel6

ADAM: "…but everything's DYING." What a great line foreshadowing what's to come.

PAGE 11

GEOFF: I wrote JUSTICE SOCIETY OF AMERICA, and the previous series JSA, when I started writing comics and had just left the series when I was moving onto starting BLACKEST NIGHT. Recently, I had taken in Damage and he'd turned into one of my favorite and most complex characters on the team. Damage is the son of the Golden Age Atom, but unlike most of the sons and daughters of the JSA, he never met his father face-to-face or cared about carrying on his legacy. BLACKEST NIGHT give me the opportunity for Damage to finally meet his father.

PAGE 12

GEOFF: Let me talk about Aquaman's wife and Queen of Atlantis, the enigmatic Mera. Her origin is a bit undefined. She's from "another water dimension" and she showed up early in the AQUAMAN series. She was the one character in the DC Universe that didn't appear to have any real connection or role in BLACKEST NIGHT, but I knew from the beginning that I didn't want to only focus on the obvious or focus on a smattering of everyone. But Mera, in my opinion, has the potential to be one of the strongest female heroes in the DC Universe. She was clearly the breakout of BLACKEST NIGHT...maybe next to Larfleeze.

ALEX: Aquaman has always been one of my favorites, but I had never colored Mera before. I love textures so she became one of my favorite characters in the series and Ivan did an amazing job drawing her (and everyone else)!

PAGE 12/panel 1

NICK: Did a lot of tombstones during this series (might have a second career there :)), but Aquaman's was tough.

PAGE 12/panel 5

IVAN: Death has already arrived to the sea.

PAGE 14-15

IVAN: I love to draw multiple images of the Flash to show his fast movements... even to show the simple ones.

PAGE 16-17

ADAM: An incredible, overwhelming spread beautifully illustrated by Ivan Reis showcasing the many deaths that have occurred in the DC Universe.

IVAN: I think it was more than 55 characters.

GEOFF: This and the following page are my favorite moments in the first issue, and they tie directly into my favorite moment in issue #8.

ALEX: I have a version of this without the Green Lantern construct effect over it because "you never know."

NICK: This is what a letterer calls a "gimme" page—SILENT—but man, I stared at this one a while. Are they all dead? Beautiful, Ivan!

PAGE 18

EDDIE: This page is a testament of Ivan's artistic abilities. He totally sells how sad Barry is over the loss of his friends.

PAGE 19

IVAN: The first time we see Hawkman in the story… I love drawing Hawkman.

PAGE 22/panel 1 and 2

IVAN: This is the only moment that you can see Flash sitting down with no additional movement. He just learned about all his dead friends and he's devastated.

PAGE 26/panel 1

ADAM: My favorite panel possibly in the entire series. This is where things turn and really get bad. What an image! Scar takes a bite out of a Guardian and we're off to the races.

GEOFF: Definitely a horror moment but not the most heart-wrenching of issue #1.

PAGE 30-31

EDDIE: Pretty much Guy said it all. Things were gonna get nasty.

IVAN: Everybody in this spread is dressed in black costumes with heavy shadows on their faces and black borders on the page…I don't know how it was possible to discern all the characters =)

PAGE 30-31/panel 2

NICK: Man! This is when you say to yourself, "How can I put a huge piece of text on this freakin' magnificent piece of art"? The "RISE" was a big commitment for this page. Seems to have worked out.

PAGE 30-31/panel 3

NICK: THIS is when I realized that J'onn was coming back and not in a "feel good" way. I also realized there were no limits to where Geoff would take this story. I was HOOKED!

PAGE 33

NICK: "GET OUT OF THE HOUSE! THE CALL'S COMING FROM INSIDE THE HOUSE!!" Anyone who can place that quote knows how on the "edge of my seat" I was during this scene.

PAGE 33/last panel

EDDIE: The nascent "Black Lantern vision" that would become so prevalent over the series and give it a unique flavor.

GEOFF: Eddie, this is an important thing to pull out. The creative coordination that BLACKEST NIGHT required only worked because of Eddie and Adam. Eddie, in particular, really focused on ensuring that the "Black Lantern vision" was present in every tie-in and series. Plus it looked cool. We refined the look in the subsequent GREEN LANTERN issue that followed this one.

PAGE 35/panel 2

ALEX: My face looked just like Hawkman's when I opened this page. This whole sequence really stuck with me for a while after I finished it. Geoff and Ivan skillfully depicted so much emotion here.

PAGE 40/panel 3

JOE: For me the most terrifying moment and the one that set the tone for the whole Blackest Night was the Hawks being attacked by Ralph and Sue Dibny. That was cruel, ruthless and heartbreaking at the same time. When at last Carter and Kendra are about to be together, they die! Just heartbreaking!

GEOFF: Originally, when I was first laying out the series, I had thought somewhere Hawkman and Hawkgirl would be killed by their own bodies, but when they became the first ones murdered by the Black Lanterns I knew the scene had to be more. I also knew how "evil" it was to have the corpses be the Elongated Man and Sue Dibny. But for me, it was more horrific because they were such a sweet couple who had such a tragic ending – which is what the Hawks unfortunately are cursed with: to meet and fall in love in every life and die at the height of it.

OCLAIR: Dude, I can't highlight a specific point that is my favorite here. The story develops at such a crazy pace, culminating on the last page! And then... we want MORE!

ISSUE #2

PAGE 1

IVAN: With the dead rising, the story opens in widescreen.

PAGE 6/panel 1

GEOFF: Issue #2 was an always going to be about building tension, dread and centered around Black Lantern Aquaman's reveal. I wanted to anchor the issue around who I considered our main dead hero. I see Aquaman as one of DC's toughest heroes, dead or alive.

ADAM: Here's our first shot of Black Lantern Aquaman and holy cow, he just ripped out the heart of one of his people. Our heroes are evil and they kill. ANYTHING can happen!

ALEX: He's undead, he's evil...but he is still sooooo cool looking.

OCLAIR: Again a crazy rhythm here that culminates in Aquaman's appearance! The carnage begins, and it ends with Garth's death! Even the "calm" (if that's an adjective I can apply here) parts, such as the Phantom Stranger/Black Lantern Spectre is crazy! Every page I inked got me looking forward to what would happen next!

PAGE 7

NICK: This page took a while... Second time I had to do the "Black Lantern Oath" (First was in the #0 issue) had to make sure to help bring the reader around the page as Geoff & Ivan intended-PLUS-C'mon! It's the Black Lantern Oath! DON'T CHOKE!

PAGE 7/panel 2

NICK: Deadman in the fetal position, rocking (Oh! The page doesn't move but I know he's rocking!) repeating: "Stay Dead! Stay Dead!" MAJOR CREEPY! Nice scene, guys!

GEOFF: I've said it before (well, on Twitter) but Nick rocked it this whole series. Lettering is an art form all its own because it's incorporated into Ivan's art, especially scenes like this. Placement, font, size can make or break a page. Especially when I write too much dialogue!

PAGE 7/next to last panel

ADAM: "I don't WANT to come back." He doesn't know how correct he is but that's for another story.

JOE: I can't wait to see that!

BLACKEST NIGHT DIRECTOR'S COMMENTARY

PAGE 8/panel 3

GEOFF: This was another important moment for me. The only character that the black rings are unable to corrupt postmortem is Don Hall, Dove. Dove was the avatar of peace. He's content that he's lived his life and has fully accepted that he's dead. He also shares something in common with the white light, as Dawn Granger the second Dove does. Exactly what is another story we're telling in BRIGHTEST DAY.

PAGE 11/panel 3

ADAM: What a great idea to have Aquaman be able to control dead sea life. Great one, Geoff! And check out Ivan's amazing rendition. What an amazing fight scene. Check out that eel ripping off the Atlantean's lips.

GEOFF: Although BLACKEST NIGHT is dark, I still wanted it to be fun. And what's more fun than zombie sharks?

PAGE 12/panel 5

ADAM: I LOVE Pariah. You always knew something awful was going to occur when he showed up, so I knew Geoff had to put him in here and what a way to do so.

PAGE 14-15

ADAM: The double page vertical spread really showcases the immense size and power of the Spectre, and we know we're in massive trouble.

ALEX: I just love how Ivan drew him "muscles out" as if the skin has been removed. Great image!

IVAN: Yep! I took off his skin... just to show the muscle... he could join in the Body World Expo.

ADAM: Who's been pumping Crispus full of steroids?

JOE: Funny thing here was you guys asked me to design the Black Lantern Spectre and I thought... "Wow! Cool! Jim Corrigan as a Black Lantern!" I did the design and just then you told me it should be Crispus Allen!

GEOFF: Should it be...?

PAGE 18

IVAN: Here we discover that we can't kill the dead.

PAGE 19/ panel 1

EDDIE: This was an especially hard scene for me as a Titans fan and a fan of the underdog that Garth was. But these deaths had to mean something, and the demise of the original Aqualad had a big impact that will continue to affect the living characters.

GEOFF: I knew how much a fan Eddie was of Tempest and we also knew if someone died in BLACKEST NIGHT it was no longer going to be mean that they were coming back next issue. Although twelve do at the end (spoilers!), the rest are dead.

PAGE 24

EDDIE: What can you say, but wow and look out, heroes.

ALEX: I did my best to keep scenes with regular heroes clean and slick and anything with Black Lanterns really textured and decayed—hard to look at. This page is a good example of just how much texturing I tried to get away with.

ISSUE #3

PAGE 1

EDDIE: Originally, this scene opened with Gen and Jason making out. I wanted more of a cliché teen horror movie opening with these two. We went back and forth on it. Ivan eventually drew the more serious version, which with everything else that winds up happening I think turned out for the best—this was just not a slasher flick.

GEOFF: Yeah, in all honesty, I think this was the one scene that was re-written to have them making out, but the revised script got lost and Ivan drew from the original. We all decided it worked best anyway.

PAGE 4/panel 3

ALEX: I just want to say how freaking cool this panel is. So chilling it's almost hard to look into his eyes.

PAGE 6/panel 1

ADAM: The Atom popping out of the black ring is a freakin' awesome idea, Geoff. And look at the ripped mask and black eye, he sure got in a massive scrape with Hawkman and Hawkgirl.

PAGE 10

EDDIE: OK, this is a perfect example of a cool character just breaking out. Mera was not intended to have such a huge part in this, but she started commanding every scene she was in.

PAGE 11/panel 4

ADAM: Some more foreshadowing here. Ray Palmer is glowing with Compassion. Hmm…

NICK: I hadn't figured out the emotional tether at this point. I figured Ray (The Atom) was gonna bite it here!

GEOFF: The Atom is another example of a character seemingly with no connection to BLACKEST NIGHT but ends up becoming a vital part of saving the universe from Nekron.

PAGE 12/panel 1

EDDIE: And here's Indigo! She just burst onto the scene. I don't think anyone ever considered how bad-ass compassion could be.

ADAM: Or how mysterious!

OCLAIR: Here we start to have a little hint of what's waiting for us ahead. And a little hope is installed in our little hearts!

NICK: AND – RAY LIVES!!

PAGE 14/panel 1

IVAN: And here we discover we CAN kill the dead. =)

GEOFF: I wanted to set up the rules clearly on how you kill a Black Lantern. After two issues of seemingly unstoppable undead heroes and villains, Indigo-1 revealed the secret behind it — it takes a combined force of two powers from the emotional spectrum. And with the Indigo Tribe able to channel others in the immediate area, they make strong allies in this fight. Their ultimate mission, however, remains a mystery.

NICK: As much as I love Ralph & Sue — after they slaughtered the Hawks in issue one I was still SOOOO ticked. They had to go—BIG TIME!

JOE: I loved that document you guys created for all creators working on BLACKEST NIGHT tie-ins. All the rules on how to kill those damn bastards!

PAGE 15/panel 5

EDDIE: One little panel sets up the trouble the deceased Detroit League would be to the JLA in their book.

PAGE 16-17

EDDIE: Another of Ivan's amazing vertical spreads that would become the signature of the series. Our wonderful Brazilian artist would top himself with each one.

NICK: Agreed, Eddie. We worked really hard to get Indigo's dialogue to overlap with the relevant panels.

PAGE 16-17/panel 4

NICK: See those "Please Standby"s behind Hal? Eddie and Adam asked me to put them everywhere in this book! Obsess much, guys?!

ADAM: We love ya, Nick!

PAGE 24

EDDIE: Like I said, this was no simple zombies attack/slasher flick. Underscoring it was the emotional content that would also tear at the readers' heart too. Nice job, Geoff.

ADAM: A real gut-wrenching scene. Geoff wanted this to be a few pages long to really pull at your emotions and boy, did it work.

IVAN: And it was the same camera sequence for four pages… just with emphasis on the emotions of the characters and Geoff's terrific script.

NICK: TORE—MY—HEART—OUT!! Man, you guys are hard. Was kind of hoping we might see her at the (bright) end—didn't work out that way.

JOE: This issue was the one I started helping Oclair Albert on the inks. It was the testing ground for me on how to ink Ivan, and at the same time make it look as good as Oclair's inks. Tough job! I love this whole sequence because the emotional content was so heavy!

ADAM: What a terrific job you did on the series, Joe! Over 100 designs and the spectacular inks all made for an unbelievable BLACKEST NIGHT event.

GEOFF: This was the hardest death scene I ever wrote. The torture is not only on Gen, but Jason. I knew this was going to have major fallout well beyond BLACKEST NIGHT and into BRIGHTEST DAY after Ronnie Raymond returned. Firestorm, like Aquaman and Martian Manhunter, is one of DC's mainstays in my opinion and deserves some more spotlight in the center of the DCU.

ISSUE #4

PAGE 2-3

EDDIE: Ivan's take on Black Lantern Copperhead was so cool, we gave him the cover focus on this issue.

ALEX: Yeah, he's also the only Black Lantern with a tad more color on him than anyone else. Eddie had his favorites.

EDDIE: Yeah, but originally, I thought we'd have more color on the BLs like with Aquaman. You got off easy, Sinc.

NICK: NOT THAT WAY, BARRY!!

GEOFF: Hahahahaha!

PAGE 4/panel 2

ADAM: Notice that since Jason Rusch is inside Firestorm and his emotions are running rampant, that the power levels are still increasing. But what will happen when they reach 100%?

NICK: This scene was a classic "Indiana Jones running from the boulder"! AWESOME. Only difference is Barry's trying to save Mera and Ray along the way! OH—and the boulder is ZOMBIES!

PAGE 8/panel 3

GEOFF: I knew that readers would feel like this scene was "out of place" initially until I revealed that both Scarecrow and Lex Luthor would play bigger rolls in the series later on. I wanted to set up Scarecrow's lust for fear and his inability to feel it because of his years of exposure to fear gas…unless hunted by the Batman.

ADAM: The Scarecrow shows no emotion in Black Lantern vision so Azrael cannot see him. This is due to the fact that he's immune to terror and sets up the role he'll be playing later on in this book. It'll be the greatest feeling he'll ever have.

ALEX: Black Lantern Azrael was one of my favorite BL designs—awesome job, JOE!

JOE: It was awesome designing Black Lantern Azrael!

PAGE 12

EDDIE: This scene crystalized who our next big stars would be, but also reminded us that Barry Allen, The Flash is cool!

JOE: A whole new "Trinity" and they worked so damn well.

PAGE 20/panel 1 & 2

EDDIE: Another hero dies, and Ray Palmer is confronted with a ghost that has been haunting him for a very long time.

GEOFF: I went back and forth on who should kill Damage. The obvious idea was his father the Golden Age Atom for whom he had pent-up anger because he was absent in his life. It was a large part of the chip on Damage's shoulder. But instead I wanted a glimmer of hope. I wanted Damage to finally overcome that rage and grab onto hope for the first time maybe ever. And that, unfortunately, would not only be his downfall, but the return of Ray Palmer's greatest and strangest enemy…his ex-lover and murderer of Sue Dibny, Jean Loring.

PAGE 22/panel 1

IVAN: Here starts Nekron's rise, and I changed all the borders on the pages to black.

ADAM: In case you're wondering who those two Black Lanterns are, they are Ash and Saarek, who are the two Green Lanterns that were tricked into going to Ryut where the Black Power Battery lay.

ALEX: This whole sequence was awesome, culminating with the big Nekron reveal. For the Black Lantern, I wanted it to look like spirits or something supernatural was coming out of it rather than just light.

PAGE 24-25/panel 1

OCLAIR: With all the deaths and Black Lanterns showing up, can it get any worse? YES! It can! The LORD OF THE DEAD appears! Damn!

EDDIE: A version of Nekron had appeared before, but he was nothing like this. Geoff and Ivan let the dark side of their imagination loose for this creation.

GEOFF: Originally, we had planned on creating a new character, but the concept of Nekron was already within the Green Lantern mythology, although he had rarely appeared.

JOE: I remember all of us trading emails almost 'til midnight until Ivan sent the final design. That day we talked on the phone for hours exchanging ideas.

ALEX: Each final splash was more amazing than the previous one, and this one is probably my favorite. I found myself getting caught up in all the detail Ivan put into every undead body coming out of the ground. I used some overlapping fractal filters and layers to create the effect.

ISSUE #5

PAGE 2-3

ADAM: The New Guardians have arrived, and they're here to stay. I'm so excited about all these brand new characters that Geoff, Ivan and others have created. They're such a part of the Green Lantern mythos now and have such incredible personalities. And the oaths are utterly fantastic! But check out Larfleeze on the side over there wondering why these fools are wasting their time and pondering how he'll get a hold of all their rings and power batteries.

IVAN: Alex was the star of this spread, keeping the dark tone of the story with a rainbow of colors.

ALEX: I too said, "Ooooooooh…pretty," when I saw this, then I realized this was where I had to really earn my money. I had to use eight different light sources without allowing one to stand out over the others. It also couldn't look like someone just dropped a bag of Skittles on the page. Luckily Ivan drew them (unintentionally?) in cool-warm-cool-warm order so the final image did not feel unbalanced when it was colored.

GEOFF: A big part of the pride I really take in BLACKEST NIGHT as a whole is that we introduced all these new characters into the DC Universe that are here to stay. Along with reviving classic characters and reinventing ones like Black Hand and Nekron, creating characters that don't fade away is a real challenge, and with the help of my amazing artistic collaborators we did it. Obviously, I have a lot of fun writing Larfleeze, but Saint Walker may be the unsung hero and the most complex in my mind. I particularly love where we're taking him post-BLACKEST NIGHT.

PAGE 5/panel 2

ALEX: I love the Flash. I've been dying to work on him for a long time because I have always wanted to make him look like he is moving so fast that you're not really sure where he is at. I am so grateful to Ivan for allowing me to explore this with his art in this series. This panel stands out to me as a good example of how I think the Flash should look.

GEOFF: I love the way you expanded on what Ivan did with the Flash, Alex. The speed blurs and lightning that crackled around him really stood out, especially against the often black backgrounds.

BLACKEST NIGHT DIRECTOR'S COMMENTARY

PAGE 14-15

EDDIE: Ivan's contribution to Scar's final look.

IVAN: Here Scar is dominated by the scar…it's growing across her entire body…the blackness growing inside her.

EDDIE: I love this spread! Our New Guardians cutting loose on Scar. Geoff talks about moments you wanna hang up on your wall. This is one of them. Actually, with BN there's hardly any wall space left when the series is done.

ADAM: Ivan continues to blow me away. Every page that he sends in makes my jaw drop. And check out those colors from Alex Sinclair. All the light surrounding Scar rocks.

ALEX: Taste the Rainbow! C'mon, somebody had to say it. Great idea from Geoff to have the merging colored beams become pure white light. I added the multicolored streaks as a kind of color echo.

PAGE 20-21

OCLAIR: And then Black Lantern Batman appears! Even if it was just for a few pages, THAT made us fear for our heroes!

EDDIE: I was in Brazil with Ivan when he showed me this page. It's a wonder it and I ever made it back to the States.

JOE: Cool thing was that back at San Diego Comic-Con '09 I was sketching out a Black Lantern Batman just for fun, then Eddie showed up out of nowhere, saying, "Oh, awesome, Joe! Now put that away! No one needs to see that now. C'mon!" One week or so later, Black Lantern Batman was born. I also love the fact that I inked this spread!

ALEX: The funny thing about the art on this series is that you'll open the book and say, "THIS is my favorite spread." Then you find yourself saying the same thing over and over again, page after page, issue after issue. THIS is my favorite spread…until I turn the page.

PAGE 22-23

EDDIE: The emotional tether created by these pages was huge—it not only affected the characters but was visceral for all of us working on this project.

ALEX: I told you so.

PAGE 25-26

EDDIE: Yeah, this caught people off guard.

ADAM: Things have turned from bad to worse. What a twist. Go Geoff!

GEOFF: Everyone expected it to be a simple combination of light that would destroy Nekron and the Black Lantern, but the true white light was something else entirely.

ALEX: Now run along and change your underpants.

ISSUE #6

PAGE 1/panel 1

EDDIE: Love the subtle Bat-Signal shown here. A small thing, but the reason for the conflict this issue.

ALEX: And Eddie asked for more yellow on the ground to create it. I thought he was coo-coo until I tried it. Great call, Eddie!

PAGE 6/panel 2

ADAM: Ivan perfectly gets across the determination and confidence on Barry's face here as he runs forward into the future.

GEOFF: I wanted to emphasize that this was not an easy feat for the Flash…especially time-traveling without a cosmic treadmill to guide him. He and Hal could've been thrown two years into the future if he pushed himself too far.

PAGE 10-11

EDDIE: I kept rushing our colorist Alex Sinclair on this one. "What's the holdup," I said. "The Black Lanterns chasing John are all grey and black, what's the hold-up?" Aren't we editors stinkers?

ALEX: I don't think we can print what I was thinking when Eddie kept asking me that…

IVAN: You could have said something like this to me…"What's the holdup…the Black Lanterns chasing John are all a black mass with no form or details…" but you didn't… you left me to draw each one with all the details.

ADAM: And those details are what make this project far superior than anything that's come before. This really is an instant classic!

PAGE 14

EDDIE: Props to Adam for coming up with the idea of Ganthet becoming an actual Green Lantern deputy.

GEOFF: Originally, I had deputies for everyone, but I wasn't sure who would be a deputy for Green Lantern. It felt wrong to make one of our Earth heroes or villains another Green Lantern, but when we went through everyone and Adam threw out Ganthet…brilliant. This is why I love working with Eddie and Adam. Creative collaboration is the best.

PAGE 15/panels 4 & 6

ALEX: This set of panels here and on page 20 are incredible. The framing and composition Ivan used to focus on the deputy rings was so cool. I felt like I was watching a movie and the director suddenly slowed the camera down to capture that moment in time.

PAGE 19/last 3 panels

EDDIE: This could have gone different, we had other candidates for the yellow ring, but it worked out.

PAGE 20/panels 2, 4 & 6

ALEX: More of the cool framing from Ivan to emphasize those rings. Genius!

PAGE 22-23

EDDIE: And yet another shock ending. It was fun figuring out with Alex what the colors would be on these guys. Flash was hard because he looks like the Atom. Hence the huge blue lightning bolt over the Blue Lantern symbol.

ALEX: Yeah, I like the fact that we were able to incorporate colors other than their Lantern ones since they were deputies and not full-blown Lanterns. I also remember Wonder Woman's costume needed some serious surgery because the design changed after the page had been pencilled and inked.

NICK: EASTER EGG! There's art under that HUGE end caption! Show them!

OCLAIR: OK, how in hell does Luthor get an ORANGE ring??? C'mon! He's the greediest person on Earth! OK, at the end it made sense, but damn! LUTHOR???!!!

ADAM: It was also a blast figuring out which characters really embodied which emotions. We almost used the Joker.

JOE: It was awesome designing this character MONTHS before we even got the script. The Joker would have been sooo cool!

GEOFF: But it's great to give Scarecrow the spotlight. If anyone is about fear beyond Batman, it's Scarecrow, not the Joker. What's the color for insane?

ISSUE #7

PAGE 2-3

EDDIE: The penultimate chapter and all hell is breaking loose— this is why we read comics!!!!

JOE: HELL YEAH!!!

NICK: Scarecrow's having WAY too much fun with his new toy!

IVAN: And it is why the penciller doesn't sleep… I'm wrong…the spread on 10-11 is why the penciller doesn't sleep. LOL.

PAGE 7

EDDIE: Lex turns on the guys. Genius! Both on Lex's part and Geoff's for thinking of it. It should never be too easy on the heroes, and villains have to stay in character.

GEOFF: I always knew giving any kind of power to Lex Luthor was a bad idea…and I knew he had to betray the New Guardians, which was prophesized. Atrocitus even attacked Larfleeze and mentioned it in a previous GREEN LANTERN issue.

PAGE 10-11

EDDIE: Aw, hell YEAH! The colored Corps joined together. We've been talking about it for a while now and here is the moment finally. Thank you, Ivan!

NICK: Agreed! Guy's balloon should say: "Ivan makes us look GOOD!"

JOE: I remember Ivan yapping away about this for months!

GEOFF: How Ivan pulls this off, I'll never know. There is literally no one else in comics who has this kind of range. From the emotion of Carter dying and calling to Kendra to this epic spread.

IVAN: (starting to take a needed nap): ZZZZZZZZZZZZZZZZZZZZ!!!!!!!!!!!!

PAGE 14/panel 4

ADAM: The Anti-Monitor is being used to power the Black Lantern power battery and he's still in there. Uh oh!

PAGE 16/panel 5

ADAM: What insane ritual is Black Hand completing using the guts of a Guardian? Notice that the Guardian's insides make up all the colors of the spectrum, and also make note of the symbol drawn on the ground. Something is coming and it will remain in the DC Universe for a long time.

GEOFF: I wanted the Guardians' organs to literally be the seven emotions hardened like fossils inside their bodies. They had buried them so deep for so long, billions of years, they literally internalized them.

ALEX: This was a little tough to pull off. You have different colored organs—great idea by the way—covered in yellow blood and they kinda have to glow.

PAGE 18-19

EDDIE: Created over a weekend, our life Entity had to be unique.

PAGE 24-25

EDDIE: Now, this was the ending no one was expecting!

OCLAIR: Sinestro empowered by the life Entity!

ADAM: Most people believed a White Lantern would appear in BLACKEST NIGHT. Everyone thought it might be Hal Jordan who had already used some of the color rings, but lo and behold, it's the renegade Sinestro.

JOE: YEAH! Save for a few guesses here and there, almost no one was betting their chips on Sinestro. Plus it was a blast for me to create the design. After six to seven versions, we ended up going back to the first one I came up with. Fun times!

ADAM: I want to give a special shout-out to the "Greatest Letterer in the Universe" as Nick J. Napolitano has been dubbed. He's been able to create unique balloon designs for many of the characters and makes sure to highlight all of Ivan's art by taking up the least real estate as possible.

NICK: Thanks much—I'll tell ya—when this scene was building (from page 23) the way Geoff wrote it and Ivan drew it, it just swept you in. As Sinestro was imbued with the White Light, he seemed (REALLY) to be going mad. Before I even read the end caption (Beware his Power) I thought—WE—ARE—SCREWED!!

ALEX: Nick RULES!! Oh, and coloring the White Lantern for the first time was way cool. Had to mess with the logo too as the design changed over a period of time.

GEOFF: It's amazing how one TO BE CONTINUED caption can change the tone of the book – BEWARE HIS POWER.

IVAN: It was a beautiful moment... Alex was able to create a terrific atmosphere and he just used white color...all I needed to do was draw only one character.

NEXT! BEWARE HIS POWER!

ISSUE #8

PAGE 2-3

IVAN: A classic fight of the good against the evil …the black against the white.

ALEX: How cool is this spread? The classic good vs. evil/white vs. black (although with a twist since Sinestro's wearing white) image. There's so much energy and movement in this image. I had a blast on it.

GEOFF: I think, for me, this is where the entire purpose of life vs. death comes into view. It's more than just a concept to me personally; it's a personal struggle due to the loss I've had in my life. We have to embrace life the best way we can.

PAGE 6/panel 1

ADAM: Nekron is not so easily killed. He can come back as any Black Lantern. Just how powerful is Nekron? The answer might never be known.

PAGE 10-11

OCLAIR: Here all goes to hell! Everyone (I mean EVERYONE) fights against Nekron's army of Black Lanterns!

ADAM: SPEECHLESS! Just unbelievable. Ivan drew more characters on this spread than he's probably ever drawn. Let's hear from the mastermind behind it himself.

IVAN: I just didn't have the courage to count, Adam… But it was the most entertaining page I have ever done… I avoided making the aura energy around the GLs because this page had too much information and details…this way I could keep the atmosphere of the page intact.

EDDIE: At this point in any event, the artist starts to look for short cuts. Less backgrounds or none. Silhouettes. Not Ivan. He asked for more. He and Geoff would not relent!

PAGE 16-17

ADAM: The heroes strike back! A hero never gives up, they always fight back and have the resolve to continue to keep fighting even through the toughest and darkest times. This is their moment!

ALEX: New problem—buncha heroes wearing white, shooting white beams in front of a white logo. I was starting to suspect Geoff and Ivan didn't like me…

PAGE 20

ADAM: Crap! The Anti-Monitor's back. The power battery's been destroyed and there's no source powering it, but one of the greatest threats the universe has ever faced is back. When he will strike, we'll just have to wait and see.

GEOFF: Oh, you know where and when…

IVAN: …but it was a terrific moment for the Anti-Monitor.

PAGE 22-23

IVAN: Now, the big evil was defeated and the borders of the pages return to white again as the widescreen panels end… the story returns to normal panels as it was at the beginning of the series.

PAGE 24-27

ADAM: Now this warrants a gatefold poster shot! Twelve returning characters. What does this mean? Heroes and villains. Why were they chosen? What will they do with a second chance? Brightest Day is upon us, but it's not what you think.

JOE: So freakin' awesome! We've talked about a possible gatefold for months and Ivan, Oclair and Alex kicked ass on this! The hardest part for me was coming up with the designs for the heroes and villains. Tons of notes from Geoff, Pete, Eddie and Adam. These twelve characters were WAAAAY tougher to design than the 130+ Black Lanterns I came up with. Just J'onn J'onnz had fourteen different versions.

NICK: Kinda like I mentioned for issue #1—The "LIVE!" caption had a lot of weight for the narrative here (DON'T COVER IVAN'S ART) and with the heroes that were resurrected on this page it felt — historic. I was really happy with the end result. AND I didn't cover (too much of) Ivan's art.

IVAN: It was my first gatefold ever!

GEOFF: The fact that this could become a gatefold like this was wonderful – and it was Ivan's idea. We didn't have 60 pages, but when you have a moment like this that's this big, I felt extremely comfortable with 40 pages for the finale. Much to everyone's dismay, I love more pages! Many of our GREEN LANTERN issues were 24. (Sorry, guys!)

ALEX: For you techno enthusiasts, this file was a whopping 3.5 GIGs open. Took 15 minutes just to save. I was suddenly transported to the early '90s coloring on a Performa! To save time, I copied out each character, colored him/her on his/her own and pasted it back to the main file. Doing the special effects took an entire afternoon/evening.

EDDIE: It also had to be done before the rest of the book. Doing gatefolds like this is about as easy as killing Black Lanterns, but in both cases the result is well worth it.

PAGE 28/panel 3

ALEX: I love how this panel turned out. The red disappearing as her true form emerges.

PAGE 35/panel 1

ADAM: Barry searching for Ralph and Sue Dibny is an awful moment that just tears at your heart. Ivan perfectly portrayed it here. It's just so sad seeing some terrible people returned to the land of the living while some saints remain dead.

GEOFF: Tying right into that first moment of Barry realizing they're gone in issue #1. Despite everything, that pain is still there.

PAGE 40/last panel

JOE: Awesomely epic and inspiring… but what awaits our heroes in the future? Just keep reading!!!

EDDIE: Thank you, Joe, for helping with the "camera" angle here. Really makes the Lantern stand out.

ALEX: Can't wait to read what comes next!

GEOFF: It's in a vault in my office, but it'll be on stands soon!

EDDIE: I really HATE that it's over… this series had one of the best and hardest-working crews I've ever had the pleasure to be associated with!

IVAN: WOW… I hope all the readers enjoyed all the hard work spent on this story… there was so much energy and dedication put in from each of us to make sure it was the best it could possibly be… I wish the best to this team. Thanks guys… now if you'll excuse me… I'm going to slee …ZZZZZZZZZZZZZZZZZZZZZ

BLACKEST NIGHT – Deleted Rainbow Raiders Scene
By Geoff Johns

PAGE ONE
PANEL ONE.
Cut to the hidden safe house of the D-grade super-villain group: the RAINBOW RAIDERS.
They are all in a penthouse adorned with color artwork, most of which they stole, overlooking
Keystone City. It's raining outside. Lightning streaking across the sky from right to left –
like the Reverse-Flash's symbol.

RED is the leader here. All the Rainbow Raiders – ORANGE, YELLOW, GREEN, BLUE,
INDIGO and VIOLET – are gathered together. They each hold a glass full of red liquid
poured from a decanter at a nearby bar.

1. BANNER: Keystone City
2. CAPTION: The black market art gallery of the Rainbow Raiders.
3. YELLOW: We never even had a chance to take on any of the Flashes, Red. I never did.
4. RED: Do you really think we would've WON? We picked up and divided the gear of one
of the most disrespected Rogues in the business, guys.
5. RED: We're LUCKY we're not rotting away in Iron Heights, but let's all face it, it was
only a matter of time.
6. RED: If there WAS time left.

PANEL TWO.
The Rainbow Raiders all raise their glasses in a toast, high in the center of the seven
low-grade villains.

7. RED: The dead are taking over the Earth.
8. RED: Here's to being on the winning side.
SFX: klink

PANEL THREE.
The Rainbow Raiders drink the cyanide-laced Kool-Aid.

[NO DIALOGUE.]

PANEL FOUR.
An overhead shot of the seven Rainbow Raiders all lying on the ground dead a la
JONESTOWN.

[NO DIALOGUE.]

PANEL FIVE.
Same exact panel as panel four. No black rings are coming. These guys don't have any
connections to anyone.

9. CAPTION (FLASH): "As far as we know, only the dead with emotional ties to us are
rising. The rest are staying in their graves."

BLACKEST NIGHT – Deleted Ragman Scene
By Geoff Johns

DOUBLE PAGE SPREAD
PANEL ONE.
We're in Gotham City, opening on a large shot of THE RAGMAN racing frantically across the rooftops. Think of Ragman as a cross between Spider-Man, Spawn and rooted in Joe Kubert horror (who created him) rather than the clean super-hero version we've seen lately. Ragman's panicked and tired. He's in mid-leap here, off the edge of a building, over a barbed wire fence and into a massive trash yard. Something is chasing him.

1. BANNER: Earth.
2. CAPTION (BLACK HAND): I hear death call his name.
3. NEKRON (DISEMBODIED): Rory Regan.
4. CAPTION (BLACK HAND): The Ragman. He sees trash for treasure, lives in self-imposed poverty and clutches to the Kaballah in some misguided hope to cure our society of its inequity.
5. CAPTION (BLACK HAND): But despite what he believes, not everyone was created equal.

PANEL TWO.
Ragman lands hard on the huge piles of trash, losing his balance and toppling over.

6. CAPTION (BLACK HAND): It's called the food chain.
7. RAGMAN: NNFFGG
8. BLACK HAND (O/P): Your suit is an ancient patchwork prison of people stitched together by your vengeance. Each RAG a different TRANSGRES-SOR you've stolen.
9. BLACK HAND (O/P): You may be their jailer, Rory Regan –

PANEL THREE.
Ragman gazes up and we reveal a swarm of dozens of black rings flying over the edge of the building and down at him. They're like a crazed flock of birds, moving at odd angles, but then correcting their path as they lock back into Ragman and heading right for him. They burn through the barbed wire fence and any trespassing signage it might have. Nothing can keep them out.

Standing on the edge of the building where the rings are coming from is Black Hand, holding Bruce Wayne's skull.

10. BLACK HAND: -- but WE are their masters. And we want your inmates back.
11. BLACK RING: Flesh.
12. BLACK RING: Flesh.
13. BLACK RING: Flesh.
14. BLACK RING: Flesh.
15. CAPTION (BLACK HAND): Rory Regan is like the others the voice sends me after. Those who have manipulated and escaped death.

PANEL FOUR.
CUT TO the Black Lantern Hawks from pages 2 and 3 panel 2 from BLACKEST NIGHT #3. Any angle of them tackling Green Lantern Hal Jordan while the rest of the Black Lantern Justice League battle Barry Allen in the background.

16. NEKRON (DISEMBODIED): Carter Hall and Kendra Saunders.
17. BLACK LANTERN HAWKMAN: I'd rather be spilling Green Arrow's blood, but I'll settle for YOUR pompous ass, Jordan.

PANEL FIVE.
CUT TO an image from BLACKEST NIGHT: BATMAN #2 of BLACK LANTERN DEADMAN.

18. NEKRON (DISEMBODIED): Boston Brand.

PANEL SIX.
From BLACKEST NIGHT #2, the Black Lantern Spectre reaches his massive hand into the cemetery and tears it up, tossing Phantom Stranger, Zatanna and Blue Devil into the air.

19. NEKRON (DISEMBODIED): Crispus Allen.
20. BLACK LANTERN SPECTRE: You are not Hal Jordan. I have no interest in you.

PANEL SEVEN.
Black Hand approaches Ragman, but the focus is Ragman. Ragman is surrounded by the swarm of black rings like a swarm of killer bees. His rags react, shimmering and fluttering at the proximity of the black rings. There are so many balloons they should overlap one another (the names are actual DC characters, people Ragman has killed in his series).

21. NEKRON (DISEMBODIED): Cyrus Gold.
22. NEKRON (DISEMBODIED): Kit Freeman.
23. NEKRON (DISEMBODIED): Mitchell Shelley.
24. NEKRON (DISEMBODIED): Jim Craddock.
25. BLACK HAND: They will play with your essence no more.

PANEL EIGHT.
And like that, the black rings each shoot down into one of the patches on Ragman's uniform. Ragman buckles down in a standing fetal position in pain. The balloons should overlap a bit as these are not DC characters, just normal people that Ragman has incarcerated.

26. BLACK RING: Aaron Haaland of Earth.
27. BLACK RING: Jack O'Mullane of Earth.
28. BLACK RING: Jason Blanchard of Earth.
29. BLACK RING: Chaz Simmons of Earth.
30. BLACK RING: Dann McNerney of Earth.
31. BLACK RING: Lauren Howes of Earth.
32. BLACK RING: Andrew Westin of Earth.

PANEL NINE.
And then Ragman arches open as the tattered suit rips apart and the patches transform into dozens of Black Lanterns, revealing the naked, battered and smoldering Rory Regan underneath.

33. BLACK RING: RISE.
34. RAGMAN (BURST): AARRRRR!!

PANEL TEN.
VERY CLOSE ON Black Hand, pleasured from all of this.

35. CAPTION (BLACK HAND): All of this death.
36. BLACK HAND: Mm.

NEKRON

ALTER EGO: LORD OF THE DEAD
NEKRON, THE LORD OF THE DEAD, DRAWS HIS POWER FROM THOSE WHO HAVE PERISHED. HE IS THE CREATOR OF THE BLACK RINGS AND RULER OF THE LAND OF THE UNLIVING. HIS ULTIMATE GOAL IS TO DESTROY ALL LIFE, RETURNING THE UNIVERSE TO PURE DARKNESS.

Designs by Ivan Reis

THE ENTITY

ALTER EGO: TRESPASSER / WHITE LIGHT
THE ENTITY IS THE WHITE LIGHT THAT
GAVE BIRTH TO THE UNIVERSE. IT IS
ALIVE ON EARTH BUT NEEDS TO BE
CONTROLLED BY A HOST. NEKRON
BELIEVES THE ENTITY IS TRESPASSING
ON DARKNESS AND MUST BE
DESTROYED. THE ENTITY WILL DO
ANYTHING TO PROTECT LIFE.

Designs by Ivan Reis

WHITE LANTERN SINESTRO

ALTER EGO: THAAL SINESTRO
ONCE THE GREATEST GREEN LANTERN, SINESTRO WOULD BECOME HAL JORDAN'S GREATEST FOE AND FOUNDER OF THE YELLOW LANTERN CORPS. WHEN SINESTRO REALIZES THE ENTITY REQUIRES A HOST, HE STEPS FORWARD SAYING THAT HE, NOT HAL JORDAN, WILL CLAIM THE ENTITY'S POWER. SINESTRO THEN ENTERS THE WHITE LIGHT AND EMERGES A WHITE LANTERN.

Designs by Joe Prado